PREMA KIRTAN

Journey into Sacred Sound

PREMA KIRTAN

Journey into Sacred Sound

PRANADA COMTOIS

Chandra Media

Other Books by Pranada Comtois

Wise-Love: Bhakti and the Search for the Soul of Consciousness
Bhakti Shakti: Goddess of Divine Love
Exploring Bhakti: An Introduction to the Heart and Soul of Yoga
The Inner Loving Self: Finding our Highest Potential

Published by Chandra Media
an imprint of Arts of Vaishnava Culture
St. Augustine, FL United States
artsofvaishnavaculture.org

ISBN 978-1-7378914-3-7 (Paperback Edition)
ISBN 978-1-7378914-4-4 (eBook Edition)
Library of Congress Control Number: 2022930246

Design and layout by
Raghu Consbruck and Govinda Cordua
eighteyes.com

Praise for Prema Kirtan

Prema Kirtan brings out the beauty and power of kirtan in a unique poetic way that makes you fall in love with this form of expression and cultivation of devotion to the Divine. Explaining the pillars of Bhakti tradition and its meaning, these pages draw you into the mysticism of sound, the transformative power of mantra, as well as the roots and the mood of kirtan. As a kirtan singer, I am grateful to Pranada Comtois for the deep study and intricate detail, yet her insight and accessible language make this work relevant for both experienced kirtan lovers and those new to this practice.

Ananda Monet
international kirtan artist

Prema Kirtan is a well-researched, in depth, heartful study of the inner journey of kirtan, as a spiritual practice, a form of yoga, and a meditation on sound. The book is both a primer for those just discovering kirtan, as well as a wealth of knowledge for those already in the world of kirtan who want to deepen their practice.

Baird Hersey
author of *The Practice of Nada Yoga*

Pranada Comtois has gifted us again through her flowing, delightful, and insightful writing with yet another intelligent and definitive expression; this time on the intriguing subject of kirtan – the ancient spiritual practice consisting of ardent glorification and loving solicitation of the Divinity through the chanting of sacred mantra. Contextualized for the modern reader and using accessible language *Prema-Kirtan: Journey into*

Sacred Sound delivers ample enrichment and a joyful framework for progress. It is written with precision, clarity, and practical application in mind. Far more than an academic treatise – this book is a statement issuing from some four decades of intense devotional practice and research. Whether one is new to kirtan, or an experienced chanter, or simply a curious seeker, this beautiful book will prove to be a powerful, illuminating, and invaluable addition to your spiritual library.

Richard H. Whitehurst (Sridhara dasa)
author of *Mahamantra Yoga: Chanting to Anchor the Mind and Access the Divine*, Psychotherapist, Educator, Poet, Public Speaker, and Clinical Hypnotist

Whether you're new to kirtan or familiar with it, this book will help you go deeper into an exploration of mantra meditation. Deep transformation is possible through chanting sacred mantras and singing in kirtan and Prema Kirtan offers wisdom and guidance into this enjoyable, ancient and potent yoga practice.

Deva Premal and Miten
world-renowned mantra and spiritual song artists

One of the lasting memories I have from the film "Women of Bhakti" (2012) is of Pranada Comtois explaining that there is a special type of love that is reserved only for God, and how this differs from its worldly counterpart. But to fully understand this divine love, *prema* – the deep ocean of feeling and devotion toward the Supreme – requires lengthy expositions by devotees immersed in that ocean. In *Prema Kirtan,* Pranada Comtois provides a clear path toward fulfilling that need, first by describing the practices of *prema kirtan* by which *prema* is to be achieved, and then by offering the healing and transformative messages that lead one to the nectar of devotion.

Dr. Guy L. Beck
author of *Sonic Theology: Hinduism and Sacred Sound*

In her book *Prema Kirtan*, Pranada Comtois lays a compelling case for the art of kirtan being the centerpiece for bhakti. Drawing from holy scriptures such as the Bhagavad Gita, her devotion to Sri Krishna comes through as infectious as the bhakti she espouses. This work belongs in every kirtan lover's library and every bhakta's heart.

Russill Paul
author of *The Yoga of Sound: Tapping the Hidden Power of Music and Chant*

With kirtan popularity continuously on the rise, this book offers valuable insight into the tradition, the application and importance of the sacred practice of kirtan. I highly recommend all kirtan lovers to check this out!

Radhika Das
international kirtan artist

In her latest book *Prema Kirtan*, Pranada Comtois explores how sound creates a multi-faceted crystal of conscious awareness. Her journey begins with a carefully researched analysis of the influence of sound on every aspect of life. She takes her reader step by step through ever deeper understandings of the universe of sound, leading from everyday encounters inwards to the essence. She goes on to carefully guide the reader to the practice of sacred sound in the forms of mantra and kirtan.

Throughout her book are scattered gems of wisdom. Pranada Comtois devotes Chapter 5, The Yoga of Kirtan, to relating her personal experiences with kirtan and mantra. I found this most illuminating. To hear the author's personal journey brings special insight. As she says, "Each person's journey is unique."

The title, *Prema Kirtan,* has a special significance. Pranada explains that kirtan can be of two kinds. It can aim for release into the Oneness, which she calls "mukti kirtan." Or it can be an expression of pure love for Krishna, which she calls Prema Kirtan. For Pranada Comtois pure love is the goal.

Ranchor Prime
author of *The Birth of Kirtan*

Prema Kirtan is valuable for its personal reflections on the nature of kirtana, giving the reader of a picture of that it is, what it means, how it functions within community, and how it is thought about in terms of Vaishnava scripture and history. Readers will enjoy the interweaving of narrative, history, and theory in well composed prose.

Jonathan Edelmann, PhD
Associate Professor at University of Florida

Prema Kirtan is exactly what the world needs right now – a practical guide to the science and art of kirtan. This simple spiritual practice is so accessible a child can do it. Kirtan holds within it a seedling that, when planted in the heart and properly nourished, can heal and transform the world. Using her own life expressed through her gift of clear and loving language, Pranada shows us how.

Gaura Vani
kirtan artist

Prema Kirtan is a profound and unique work that is full of gems for all types of readers. Whether one is a complete beginner on the spiritual path or an experienced kirtan practitioner, they are sure to receive inspiration and insights from this work. The writing style is intricate and poetic, yet accessible and clear. Pranada's own spiritual depth and absorption in the beautiful practice of kirtan shine through in the pages. This is a must read for anyone looking for simple and practical ways to awaken more love and joy into their life.

Madhu
conscious business and lifestyle coach, international
retreat leader, and professional musician/kirtan artist

CONTENTS

For my grandchildren Meena Vilasini and Valen:
When life bears down on you, call out the Name,
when life favors you, call out the Name.
Let your heart sing pure and be happy.
May all children chant and be happy.

FOREWORD

I've known Pranada since the mid-seventies, almost as many years as I've been practicing kirtan. We are fellow travelers on the Bhakti path. I've been impressed by her keen perception and thoughtfulness. Her studies of sacred texts and her ability to explain them never ceases to amaze me. Through all the phases of her life, from the early days of practicing Bhakti in an ashram environment, to raising a family, running businesses, facing calamities and health challenges, she has remained fixed in her personal spiritual practices and studies. She is passionate to present the esoteric truths and practices of Bhakti in a way that makes them accessible to contemporary audiences new to the path. In short, I can't think of a better person to write this important book, *Prema Kirtan*.

I was introduced to the wonderful world of kirtan almost fifty years ago. I was immediately attracted. Coming from a background in music and eager to take up spiritual life, I appreciated being able to express myself through kirtan. Yoga and music together – what could be better? I was especially drawn to the singing of A. C. Bhaktivedanta Swami Prabhupada, who would become my principal guide and guru on this path. I felt something wonderful in his voice that I'd never experienced before. Gradually I came to understand that what I was hearing was pure love. There was not the slightest tinge of ego or pride. The emotion he expressed was not covered by illusion.

I began chanting with little understanding of what that pure love actually is or the great gift I had received. Still I could feel the uplifting effects. I felt a joy in my heart I'd never known before. As I took up the study of books like Bhagavad Gita and Srimad-Bhagavatam, I gradually came to understand more about kirtan. As Pranada says, "Kirtan isn't merely music."

The kirtan I was being introduced to is directly connected to the spiritual realm (*golokera prema dhana hari nama sankirtana*). Fueled by the words of the Bhakti scriptures and saints, kirtan enters our ears and gradually manifests that realm in our hearts. Kirtan is the topmost form of experiential learning.

As Pranada writes, "Reading a book doesn't let you actually taste kirtan. We can only experience the joy and spiritual attainment kirtan provides by practicing it. What knowledge can do, however, is establish a reasonable, rational basis on which to begin and continue a kirtan practice." This is no small thing. Kirtan is simple, but the deep wisdom behind it and the mindset with which we approach it are crucial in determining the result we achieve.

For those taking up a kirtan practice or those already on the path, *Prema Kirtan* is a treasure. Pranada has brought together an amazing amount of research in both the classic Bhakti texts and contemporary writings on kirtan, yoga, and personal development. *Prema Kirtan* contains valuable information from trusted sources, presented concisely and completely. It provides us with a solid foundation for an effective kirtan practice.

Another exceptional quality of this book is how Pranada shares her realization from years of consistent, dedicated kirtan practice. She has many insights from her own experience that can help deepen our own kirtan and make it more fulfilling. Her love for kirtan is infectious!

For the past thirty years I've had the good fortune to travel the world sharing kirtan. Having personally witnessed the transformative power of kirtan in my own life and in the lives of many others, I recommend this book for all those with an open mind who are looking for their highest self-interest.

Happy chanting!
Bada Haridas

INTRODUCTION

But few will hear
the secrets
hidden within the notes.
– Rumi

Three friends unexpectedly showed up in my front yard carrying a yellow rose bush, a tea olive bush, and a hydrangea plant – all gifts for my birthday. Since we hadn't seen each other for a while, we gathered in my living room to catch up. Our conversation naturally turned to sharing details of our successes and shortcomings in our daily spiritual practices. As serious decades-long practitioners of bhakti, the heart and soul of yoga, we were always receiving new insights. Long ago we'd found that sharing our experiences not only encouraged one another's cultivation of devotion but enlightened us about what worked and what didn't. It has never ceased to amaze me how rich and varied the inner journey is, how profound the bhakti philosophy, and how valuable my friends and other sincere seekers have been for my spiritual development. My thoughts drifted for a minute.

Yamuna Devi turned to me, "Please lead kirtan, Pranada."

Along with philosophical discussions, our get-togethers were always enriched by at least some time spent in kirtan. Kirtan is the musical form of bhakti-enriched mantra meditation.

Born of love, the call-and-response song using sacred mantras is the expression of the soul proper. During kirtan we call out to our Beloved in separation. The particular kirtan known as *prema-kirtan** has the power to carry us into the land of love and unite us with our Divine Other.

At Yamuna's request I hesitated. Yamuna was an exceptional singer and proficient harmonium player and had been a pioneer in bringing kirtan to the West. She'd recorded kirtan albums with George Harrison and led kirtan in front of thousands of people in Europe and India. But she always wanted others to lead the singing of kirtan, and in this way she showed how kirtan welcomes everyone.

"Oh, Yamuna," I sighed, looking at her. We both knew what I meant. She returned my glance with a look that said, "Go ahead. Sing."

So I reached for my pair of hand cymbals (*karatals*) and began singing the Hare Krishna maha-mantra.

Kirtan is also often accompanied with a *mridanga*, a double-headed barrel drum that's been played in India for more than two thousand years, and a harmonium, a portable, free-reed organ. Yamuna was an accomplished harmonium player, but today she just wanted to sing along, and I wasn't inclined to pull out any of the other instruments. So I played the cymbals to a slow *ching-ching-chiiiinnng* beat.

My friends and I do kirtan daily – sometimes alone, sometimes with a few friends, sometimes with larger groups of friends, and sometimes with hundreds of people. We also chant

---

* *Prema-kirtan* is pronounced *pray-ma–kear-ton*. The two syllables in *kir-tan* sound like the English words hear and ton. The correct spelling of this Sanskrit phrase is *prema-kīrtana,* with an "a" at the end of kirtan. However, *kirtan* has entered the West without its final "a," through the Hindi language. But *prema* is still relatively unknown, and I've decided to spell it according to the original Sanskrit – with an "a" at the end.

kirtan at events where we're introducing kirtan to those who've never experienced it. Each kirtan is a little different, but whatever the circumstances, the purpose is the same: to feelingly chant the sacred mantra petitioning our Supreme Friend with love.

As I chanted, I became self-conscious of my voice, mentally comparing it to the richness and depth of Yamuna's, but then I closed my eyes and prayed to enter into meditation on the sacred sound. I sang a mantra, and then was quiet as I allowed myself to feel embraced by my friends' singing response. After a few minutes, bathed by my deep connection with them, I opened my eyes and looked at each of my friends. Yamuna's eyes were closed, and a few tears were streaming down her cheeks. Seeing her sweet face, my heart melted.

What a beautiful, real effect of kirtan. I thought. *These profound feelings are increasing and deepening as we continue our bhakti practice, aren't they, Yamuna?*

Such private moments, when we're transported to another realm, don't appreciate intrusions, so I didn't voice my thoughts even after I brought the kirtan to a close.

Kirtan has become a popular musical genre in the West. Reaching out beyond ashrams and yoga studios, echoes of kirtan are now heard in other traditions, and kirtan is even making its way into the mainstream in other ways.

As we sit (or dance!) in conventional kirtans we hear ancient melodies, feel the lead singer's heartfelt expression, enjoy our own participation as we sing along, allow the subtle power of the mantra to work its magic, and ride on the expertise of the musicians. Kirtan causes the heart to swell with love and joy, and when we meditate on the mantra, we feel that profoundly.

People who attend kirtans describe how much the meditation uplifts and enriches them. Many people state that they feel they're tapping into a sacred space within themselves and connecting with the universal divine.

To enjoy kirtan and benefit from a kirtan practice, one doesn't need to be musically inclined or have a special voice. And most people are unaware that singing kirtan isn't dependent on others being present with them, although it's certainly special when we can share with the voices of many sincere souls. Fewer people know that there are many types of kirtan, not just musical kirtan.

What allows us to reap the harvest of a kirtan garden planted in the heart is knowledge of bhakti, the yoga of divine love, which gave birth to it. In that, this book will help you.

While many like to attend kirtans, few know of the purpose, practice, and spiritual possibilities kirtan offers, and fewer still know the special characteristics of prema-kirtan. Without knowledge of the use and nature of mantras, these participants are only able to touch the surface benefits of kirtan. Their spiritual experience can be wonderfully aided by increased familiarity with the science of kirtan. I have written *Prema Kirtan* for all those who want to enhance their understanding of prema-kirtan, *japa*,* mantra meditation, and bhakti, and to highlight how a *sadhana* (practice) of kirtan that reaches for *prema* (divine love, or paramount bliss to an absolute degree) broadens and deepens the spiritual dimension of our lives.

Within its own venerable culture in India, kirtan is part of

---

* *Japa* refers to private mantra meditation. The same mantras chanted in kirtan in a group can be chanted privately, as japa, by an individual. For a detailed description of how to chant japa and use a mala (chanting beads), see "How to Chant Japa and Use a Bead Mala" in the appendix.

a daily meditation practice. While all traditions and cultures are rich with a broad diversity of spiritual and religious music, kirtan features ancient mantras, potent sound formulas that can transform us at our core and enable us to see past illusion to spiritual truth, past the material and temporary to the permanent, past the false self to the true self. Descending from a higher plane of existence, sacred mantras brim with spiritual potency and carry news of our home. Those who are sufficiently homesick will find comfort in prema-kirtan.

So kirtan isn't merely music. Embedded within the beautiful harmonies carried by voice and instruments – or the sound of our own voice as we chant during japa – we bathe in sacred mantras that cleanse our consciousness, remove our karmic bond of action and reaction, and root out the egoic false self.

In Search of the Cradle of Civilization Georg Feuerstein lends perspective: "Self-knowledge is not mere psychological understanding, or insight into our personal or emotional history. It is not merely an exercise of our memory but knowing the singular Being as it reveals itself in and through consciousness, which is eternal and transcends all outward and transient identities, including the I-am-the-body idea, which breeds only division and death. Authentic self-knowledge is unmediated knowledge, or realization, of our true identity beyond the mind-body complex and its limitations in time and space."

Kirtan is the primary practice of bhakti yoga. It's an easy yoga practice, yet prema-kirtan promises the highest attainment of all yoga systems. That it offers an easy, friendly way for the highest aim highlights the power and generosity of the process. In *Prema Kirtan* I detail this yoga practice and make it more accessible to our Western thinking, aptitudes, and situations, drawing on my four and a half decades of personal practice.

I am initiated into the line of Sri Chaitanya Mahaprabhu, founder of prema-kirtan. The school I belong to is known as the Gaudiya Bhakti Vedanta school rooted in the teachings of the Bhagavad Gita and Bhagavata Purana (Srimad-Bhagavatam).

Those engaged in a kirtan practice are instruments to be tuned, and the mantras of prema-kirtan bring us into harmony with ourselves, others, and our Divine Source. Russill Paul writes in *The Yoga of Sound,* "In its fullest sense, yoga is a form of prayer through the conduit of our bodies."

By immersing ourselves in meditation on the mantras of prema-kirtan, our whole material existence draws to a close. The soul's dark night ends as the rising sun of prema reveals to us the security of our eternal, unchanging nature. Kirtan takes us on a full exploration of both the nature of being and Reality and brings us to blissful life in our eternal home.

Reality in this context doesn't refer to our "real life" of paying bills, going to work, taking care of children and pets, or other aspects and responsibilities we have in the physical world. Reality with a capital R draws our attention to what is unchanging and permanent, to the truth that underlies both material and spiritual existence.

Of course, reading a book doesn't let you actually taste kirtan. You can only experience the joy and spiritual attainment kirtan provides by practicing it. What knowledge can do, however, is establish a reasonable, rational basis on which to begin and continue a kirtan practice. It's experience that will open to you unmediated knowledge. The rest is in your hands – or more specifically, your heart.

May *Prema Kirtan* enrich the soil of your heart to create a favorable place to grow the seed of the bhakti creeper. If you water that seed with kirtan in the association of like-minded and sincere people, you'll find the flower of divine love blossoming. This has been the experience of countless others throughout millennia. The fragrance of the flower of divine love will madden you and draw your Divine Other to you, and it will forever relieve the fever of material desire and distress.

What Lies Ahead

I have tried to distill the essence of kirtan and mantra meditation from dozens of ancient texts on bhakti yoga and the words of many teachers, while keeping this book concise, uncomplicated, and readable. That said, I'm covering a lot of ground here. Kirtan is deceptively simple, but this powerful yoga practice is deeply rooted in a sophisticated philosophy.

I've divided the book into three parts. Part I, chapters 1–4, discuss what prema-kirtan is and its basic, philosophical foundations. I also discuss the nature and power of sound, and, in particular, of sacred sound, the driving force of kirtan. Chapter 4 introduces the main mantra of prema-kirtan and the other practices of bhakti yoga, which support a kirtan practice.

In part II, chapters 5–8, I describe the types of experiences a kirtan practitioner can expect to have, and how the mantra heals psychologically and spiritually and frees one from self-imposed limitations. I also share the benefits one can garner from practicing prema-kirtan with like-minded aspirants.

In part III, chapters 9–11, I share the origins of kirtan and how it came to the West. Chapters 10 and 11 are the most philosophical in the book. Here, I take you on a search for the perfect object of love – that person who can grant divine love – which is the goal of prema-kirtan. In chapter 11 we journey to the various destinations in the cosmic hierarchy. This information will allow readers to choose a mantra from the many mantras heard in kirtans that matches their interests and material or spiritual goals.

Part I

THE HEART
OF KIRTAN

Chapter 1

THE ALLURE OF KIRTAN

You've been walking the ocean's edge,
holding up your robes to keep them dry.
You must dive naked under,
and deeper,
a thousand times deeper.
– Rumi

The transparent, aqua-green Caribbean Sea enamored me. The aquas, turquoise blues, and emerald greens opened clear and crisp above the white sea floor. Sometimes I could stare out at the sea for hours, my breath washing in and out of me as slowly as the lazy, lapping waves.

On scuba dives I submerged into the sea's quiet, comforted by the rhythmic sound of my underwater breathing and absorbed in the kaleidoscope of colors on the living coral reefs. There I could be alone buoyed by the beauty. The underwater caves at La Caleta especially intrigued me. Making my way in the tight darkness of the hollows deep in the womb of nature reminded me of my search. I wanted illumination, but my quest had seemed to stretch on forever without light. My scuba dives kept depression at bay – I was deeply troubled that I'd come up empty-handed after an extensive investigation into an array of philosophies and spiritual paths. The sea soothed my angst.

Then, on a hot, ordinary day in Santo Domingo, I was transported beyond the beautiful expanse and dismal sadness of the world when someone led a group in chanting the Hare Krishna maha-mantra. I'd never experienced the meditative call-and-response song of kirtan before, never chanted mantras, and never considered the power of sacred sound. Of course, I'd experienced the power of music to change my feeling states, but those emotional depths always seemed to flatten quickly. Kirtan was something different.

During the slow-beating resonance of the drum, and the *ching-ching-chiiiinnng* of the cymbals, I closed my eyes to better listen to the exotic sounds and noticed that the Names in the maha-mantra seemed to dance in my heart. I felt happy. It wasn't the pull of the drum or cymbals or the engaging tune that were uplifting me. I was self-conscious, singing in a foreign language in a strange place, and was bothered by the heat of the bodies in the confined space. I couldn't put my finger on why kirtan made me happy. I hadn't yet read the sacred texts that describe the transphenomenal power of the Names, so I had no point of reference for my experience. I only knew something mystical was occurring. The Names created a harmony within me; the Names were themselves harmonious.

As the chanting continued, my mind gradually calmed, then quieted, and I settled into a deeper peace than my solitary excursions into the ocean or my precious walks among California's redwoods had ever brought. Effortlessly, I slipped into a meditative state that let the room, my body, and the other chanters fade into the background. I lost touch with time and place. It was as if I was alone with the Names; they felt closer to me than my breath or heartbeat. They opened a channel to my heart, and spirit flowed through it with its inconceivable vastness, brilliance, warmth, wonder, freedom, well-being, and harmony with all life. I felt I had finally come home. The mantra was alive – distinctly alive – and I felt the comfort of settling peacefully into an inner home and a stirring of affection for the Supreme.

So this was more than simply a joyous song. I knew ordinary song – my guitar was my closest friend – and singing my angst had always brought me comfort. The music and lyrics of the songwriters of my youth spoke to me and were meaningful. But mantra and kirtan was something that went way beyond music. Music had eased me, but kirtan transported me to an inner connection with myself and what I sensed was divinity.

The Ancient Graces the New

That was in 1974, and kirtan, the ancient mantra meditation, was new to the West. Fifty years after arriving in the West, kirtan is now popular. You can find kirtan gatherings being offered at many yoga centers, meetups, and retreats. Kirtan groups play to mainstream audiences in Los Angeles, Manhattan, Miami, and numerous other cities. Globally, there are now annual kirtan festivals you can attend. In 2004, kirtan artist Jai Uttal was nominated for a Grammy, and Krishna Das played live at the 2013 Grammy Awards.

As interest in kirtan increases, so do the number of immersion retreats and workshops that teach both mantras and the traditional instruments used in kirtan – the *mridanga* (a double-headed barrel drum), the harmonium (a portable free-reed organ, brought to India by the British), and *karatals* (hand cymbals).

Some kirtan leaders borrow chants from Judaism, Christianity, Sikhism, Buddhism, and traditional African and Native American religions, creating new forms of kirtan. Other traditions are importing kirtan-style music and meditation into their practices. Rabbi David Ingber, a spiritual leader at the Romemu Center, says, "Kirtan is one of the new technologies that is going to transform the face of the Jewish world." One can see why he makes this claim by observing the effect Kirtan Rabbi Andrew Hahn and Yofiyah are having within the Jewish community.

People from all walks of life turn to kirtan for all kinds of reasons. Kirtan practitioners include teachers, architects, marketers, mothers, fathers, engineers, technicians, businesspeople, doctors, scientists, caregivers. Some people chant to deepen their yoga practice. Some say that by regularly attending kirtans they find community and a sense of belonging. Others find kirtan fulfills a spiritual longing. Still others enjoy kirtan as musical entertainment.

In 2011, *Yoga Journal* asserted that the American kirtan revolution is "spreading a compelling form of positive, spiritual music around the country and, increasingly, the world." Several pop kirtan singers are accomplished musicians who have incorporated Western musical instruments and styles with traditional Indian instruments and mantras. There are genre-bending chants that have created New Age kirtan, Hip Hop kirtan, Jazz kirtan, and Blue Grass kirtan. I recently heard a Death Metal rendition of the Hare Krishna maha-mantra.

As I write, the Recording Academy, the organization that awards Grammys, has just announced that they have changed the category "Best New Age Album" to "Best New Age, Ambient or Chant Album," in recognition of the growing interest in kirtan (Chant) and other music used as a spiritual practice.

The Easy Meditation

In its traditional form, kirtan is a meditation discipline. Kirtan makes meditation easy, giving the mind something tangible on which to focus. Most forms of meditation offer practitioners physical and emotional benefits, and mantra kirtan offers these and more. Chanters describe a state of calm and fulfillment that continues well after the kirtan ends. There is interesting research emerging specifically on the maha-mantra, the central mantra in a prema-kirtan practice.

Dr. Viveck Baluja, a neurologist at Henry Ford Hospital in Detroit, has begun a study on the effects of the Hare Krishna maha-mantra on the brain. He writes: "The data showed that the brain is not actually restful in the so-called resting state. After chanting, however, the data showed almost no cortical activation, or brain activity. This is very interesting, because it shows that you've actually been able to calm down the brain." The only method doctors currently have to decrease brain activity is to prescribe antiepileptic drugs (AEDs), and so they use these therapeutically to treat anxiety, schizophrenia, and other such conditions. "Voluntarily decreasing your brain activity is unheard of," Dr. Baluja says. "But our findings show that we can create the same therapeutic effects of medication by chanting the Hare Krishna maha-mantra. That's very exciting."

One meditator, using the Muse device,* noted that mindfulness meditation gave him a calm score hovering around 20–50 percent over a one-year period. But when he began chanting the maha-mantra, he repeatedly got readings in the 90 percent

---

* Muse is a headband that measures brain activity through EEG sensors. The EEG signal is then converted to audio feedback and fed back to the user through headphones to aid with health and wellbeing. The manufacturer claims that wearing the Muse headband helps users reach deep, relaxed states.

range. He says, "I took measurements on many people. I know it's very difficult to achieve such high scores!"

A study, published in *Journal of Clinical and Diagnostic Research* (2019), of ICU nurses experiencing moderate to severe stress states that chanting the maha-mantra relieves stress "as evidenced by increased parasympathetic tone, cognitive function, and lowered stress hormone (serum cortisol)."

Are these results studying mantra meditation simply the effect *any* type of meditation would offer? Evidently not. One study, conducted by Dr. Fred Travis, director of the ERG/psycho-physiology lab of Maharishi University, tested the theory that the sound of Sanskrit words has *specific* physiological effects. Test subjects read several verses from the Bhagavad Gita, first in Sanskrit, then in either Spanish, French, or German. They didn't know any of the languages, though they were able to pronounce all the sounds. Dr. Travis measured brain wave patterns (ERG), heart and breath rate, and galvanic skin resistance. He found that while the participants read Sanskrit their physiology was similar to those measured during a Sanskrit mantra meditation technique, but significantly different from reading a modern language.

An article in *Psychology Today* called kirtan the "easy meditation" because it focuses and quiets the mind without the strain of having to try to empty the mind, as is required for silent meditation. The article referenced studies done by the University of West Virginia and the University of Pennsylvania that showed that kirtan (of traditional Sanskrit chants) for just twelve minutes a day can improve cognition and activate the parts of the brain central to memory. Participants also reported improved sleep, mood, and quality of life. Other researchers found kirtan reduced symptoms of depression and chronic pain.

But researchers have not yet plumbed the depths of all that kirtan offers. They haven't studied the spiritual gifts kirtan grants or how kirtan affects consciousness. They may come to these studies someday. In the meantime, we are the researchers who can conduct the experiment and report the results – and we already have many testimonies.

Shortly we'll learn why and how kirtan gives practitioners first-hand experience of the self, the true nature of the world, the characteristics of transcendental reality, and reveals our relationship with our root source, the Supreme Being. It might be difficult to measure these superhuman milestones in brain-waves or skin conductance tests, but we can see the practical manifestation of how someone is changed through a deep mantra meditation practice by examining their character and behavior – behavior impossible to fake continuously.

In *Music as Yoga,* Patrick Bernard writes, "It is universally recognized that sound has the power to draw the consciousness out of sleep, to awaken it. Who has not experienced the ringing of an alarm clock? Along the same lines, the soul asleep in the bed of the physical world can awaken to real life through spiritual sound vibration."

Yoga philosophies concur: sound can awaken in us deep states of mystical consciousness, which lead to both healing and spiritual transformation. I experienced a beginning awakening in my first kirtan, and these profound benefits are the reason kirtan has survived millennia. (We review the history of kirtan in chapter nine.) That first taste of chanting the maha-mantra made me want to uncover more about the mantra of the

Names – where does the tradition of kirtan come from? What does the maha-mantra mean? What makes kirtan so captivating? What depths can kirtan make accessible? I'm still on this quest but many answers have been revealed.

WHAT IS PREMA KIRTAN?

The only life raft here is love
and the Name.
Say it, brother,
O say the divine Name, dear sister,
silently as you walk.
Don't die again
with that holy ruby mine inside
still unclaimed.
– Hafiz

Prema-kirtan is the kirtan meditation practice that leads to the development of prema, or divine love. We find kirtan within the bhakti yoga tradition, one of the four overarching schools of yoga described in the Bhagavad Gita.

Yoga is not a religion but a way to link oneself with one's spiritual ideal and find one's origins. Further, all the metaphysical and spiritual goals human beings have defined through the ages can be pursued through the four approaches to self-realization and realization of the Divine found in the yogas. Karma yoga is a linking through action, specifically good actions that bring help and light to others; jnana yoga is linking through exhaustive study of scripture and using one's reason and logic to understand and separate the self from matter; dhyana (ashtanga) yoga turns the mind and senses inward through contemplation and meditation to find the self and link with the Divine; and bhakti yoga links through acts of devotion and service to cultivate divine love.

The yogas, though distinct, are seen as a progression of development. When karma yoga is mixed with knowledge and renunciation it becomes jnana yoga, the second stage. When jnana is mixed with meditation on the Supreme it's called ashtanga yoga, the third stage. And when that is mixed with love it becomes bhakti, the fourth stage. "The entire process, which consist of various stages, is called yoga," writes Thakura Bhaktivinoda, a nineteenth-century bhakti scholar and saint, in his commentary on the Bhagavad Gita.

Historically, each school of yoga had distinct and precise methods based on the school's philosophical premises and its desired aim. The phenomenon of one yoga school borrowing methods from another is a more recent (and questionable) practice.

The asanas and pranayama now so popular in the West are derived from the meditational yoga school, which has been largely divested of its philosophical underpinnings. An asana practice without its philosophical basis can't offer the full benefit it was designed to give and therefore can become uninteresting and dissatisfying, which explains why increasing numbers of people are seeking places to learn the philosophy of yoga.

And perhaps this is one reason why the easy, charming practice of kirtan, which is from the devotional yoga school of bhakti, is being borrowed and offered by more and more yoga teachers at studios and retreats traditionally dedicated only to asana and pranayama.

The Rudimentary Step in Yoga

Spiritual attainment is much more than finding psychophysical well-being and moral ground, but it's on these aspects that 90 percent of modern spiritual and religious teachings focus their attention – to the limited benefit of practitioners.

Yoga, expressed through its four main tracks, seeks to offer practitioners a direct, unmediated experience and realization of the timeless self, the spark of spirit that is currently hiding behind whatever mask we happen to be wearing in the form of our emotional-psychological and physical bodies. These bodies are not us, and the self has nothing to do with the many ways we have come to identify with something temporary: sex, nationality, skin color, marital status, religion, political affiliation, or any other type of membership in any other type of group.

The identities we accept based on where our physical body was born, what our body happens to be doing in terms of career or affiliations or failures or successes, and who our body is associated with are all transitory – and the same for our mind, emotions, dreams, and belief systems – they will be extinguished at death, if not before. Each time we're forced to shed an identity we grieve. We endure so much pain in our lives. If I believe I'm someone's wife, my life and identity revolve – happily or unhappily – around my relationship. When my husband dies, what does my wife-self mean anymore? It's the same if I invest my identity in a career, my health, wealth, home, or any number of attachments. Who do I become when I lose one or all of these? And what to speak of the death of my body. That loss brings the greatest torment because we're *not* supposed to die! We're *not* supposed to lose those we love! We become completely disoriented each time we're stripped of one of our false identities; these losses are completely foreign to the self, who is eternal, illumined by knowledge, and fully joyful. By this we're to learn that we who are eternal cannot be happy in a temporary world filled with temporary things. This simple common sense has been true for all beings throughout time.

If we pay attention as we search for happiness through tasting, touching, smelling, hearing, and seeing, we'll discover that we can't satisfy nonphysical needs through physical gratification. The eternal self – that transpsychological part of us that seems to remain forever unsatisfied – can't be appeased with fleeting pleasures and the ownership of things.

It's likely we've heard these points before, agree with their reasonableness, and would even like to live on this platform of common sense. What keeps us from acting on this knowledge and avoiding the suffering ignorance brings? First, the whole world is operating on the exact opposite suppositions, and to go against the current turns out to be a considerable challenge. Second, we need a practical, reliable method to get to the root of who we are. At this the yogas excel.

Western yoga practitioners are becoming increasingly aware of classical yoga's ability to reduce stress and anxiety, improve the quality of life, and keep the body fit and strong. But mental and physical health and well-being are secondary – even superficial – gains in a yoga practice. Yoga wants to take us to the very nature of our existence; it's meant to help us answer why we're here, what our purpose is. Yoga wants us to give up our bankrupt lifestyle of working, consuming products, eating, having sex, playing, and going to war (figuratively and literally) to defend our views. Instead of this confusing way of being we're shown a more compelling, uplifting, and wholesome way of life and worldview. In the effort to uplift and free us, we're repeatedly brought back to the primacy of the true self because embracing this knowledge is the rudimentary step for spiritual progress. As elemental as knowledge of the self is – and a challenge to actually realize – it is also exhilarating.

In the Bhagavad Gita Krishna describes that the soul is simply amazing. He tells us that the self exists in the present, existed in the past, and will exist in the future. That which is real, he explains, always exists. The self never dies; the soul is eternal. "I exist" is axiomatic. The self exists; we cannot deny that we exist. Therefore, the self is real.

Contemplate the possibilities. How liberated from fear and insecurities we become when we realize this! I am a unit of reality with intrinsic value and meaning far grander than any-*thing* in this world. When this light goes on we realize that to know the self and act as the self is the only way to address the root cause of all our dilemmas and torments, to clear the mind of our self-forgetting, misapprehensions, misidentifications, limitations, and, ultimately, our fear of living and being and death. We come to see that there's a more precise, permanent reality under the one that meets the eye so immediately. Life has the singular purpose to seek out and know the self and connect with our original Source, without whom we don't exist and can't find happiness.

If we can finally see beyond the illusion, if we acknowl-edge that we're suffering, if we learn through experience that no amount of material enjoyment can satisfy us, and if we want a better existence, then yoga welcomes us to take up its experiential path to spirit. For those interested in a refined understanding of consciousness and the soul's possibilities in transcendence, the yoga schools offer comprehensive knowledge and precise methodologies.

Considering the seriousness of our predicament and depth and scope of the spiritual undertaking, the Gita's statement that bhakti yoga is the supreme process of all the yogas becomes quite compelling. And it is in bhakti that kirtan is born, lives, and breathes; kirtan is the central practice of bhakti yoga. This means kirtan is the most potent way to uncouple us from matter so that we can live from the true self.

The Centerpiece of Bhakti

Most people who have practiced yoga postures for a while come to hear of the eight *angas* ("limbs") of classical yoga, beginning with yama and niyama. These form a constellation of behaviors and practices that ensure the promised goal as it's defined in classical, raja (ashtanga) yoga.

Bhakti has its own limbs, numbering nine, which I discuss in chapter five. Of all the practices of bhakti, the anga, or limb, of kirtan is primary. The goal of bhakti is to realize the self *and* unite us with our Divine Other in love (prema), and the sacred sound of prema-kirtan has the power to effect the inner changes required to achieve this goal.

And what better way to augment devotion than to sing with love for the Beloved? I think of kirtan as the joining of mantra and soul in song to make a heart connection with the Supreme. The feeling part of our chanting – the love, adoration, appreciation, yearning, tenderness, longing, and passion we try to imbue it with – is the core of the practice. Through our active involvement in the yoga process of kirtan we find our heart opens and we become full, whole, happy, content, and connected to our Source Soul. In this way kirtan is a joyous petition to the soul's worshipable Supreme.

Kirtan is a reciprocal exchange of feelings between us and the Divine Person. During kirtan, our heart and our Beloved's heart stand like two mirrors facing each other. Each mirrored heart receives the love shining from the heart of the other and reflects it back – the love shared in this reciprocity pitches love to higher and higher states – and thereby increases the absolute happiness of the lover and Beloved.

Kirtan comes from the Sanskrit root *kīrt,* meaning "name, call, recite, communicate, commemorate, celebrate, praise, glorify." In a broad sense then, kirtan is expressed in more ways than just music. It's also expressed by speaking, praying, reading, writing, or hearing about the Beloved.

Another form of kirtan is japa, or private mantra meditation, using a mala, or set of prayer beads. Mantras, utterances of numinous power and wisdom, invest kirtan and japa with the potency for spiritual enlightenment.

Prema, Divine Love

There are two liberations, or ultimate states, possible for the soul: mukti and vimukti, or the special liberation called prema.

The yoga world is familiar with mukti, which is referred to as the fourth goal of life and commonly considered the highest reach of human attainment. However, there is a confidential fifth goal, hidden within the grand corpus of the Vedas, known as prema. Divine love is a post-liberated state full of transpsychological, pure emotion.

Mukti refers to liberation, which is the permanent establishment in one's authentic spiritual self, free from all identification with the mind-body complex. Mukti is a state of direct intuition of the self and its inherent joy, but one only sees a partial representation of the self's source.

Many people think of mukti as the state when at death the soul merges into the featureless Absolute. In this state the soul becomes forgetful of its individual identity. Without the ability of self-reference, this state is something like going into an eternal, deep sleep. When we learn about prema, we'll see how mukti limits the soul's full freedom in transcendence.

In prema, one also perceives the self directly, but additionally, the soul assumes its divine body and identity and is welcomed into the personal and variegated world of spirit to engage in loving relationships with the Supreme Person and the other residents there. The emotional experience of those relationships is an indescribable astonishment of the heart.

A. C. Bhaktivedanta Swami gives the example that seeing oneself in the morning means seeing the sun as well. In fact, without seeing the sunshine no one can see him or herself. When we completely realize the self, we simultaneously know the full face of our Source. Prema exceeds the bliss of mukti because the soul also experiences the ecstasy of contact with the very form of bliss, the primordial person, Love Personified and the eternal, joyous relationships in the land beyond limitations.

Only bhakti can award prema; all other yoga systems either offer material benedictions (karma) or mukti (jnana and ashtanga). This is one reason why Krishna says in the Gita that bhakti is the culmination of all other forms of yoga.

B. R. Sridhar, a bhakti scholar and self-realized saint, points out that what is viewed as a progression up the yoga ladder from karma to jnana to dhyana to bhakti is an evolution of consciousness from exploiting the world to renouncing it to dedication and love for its Source. In this way, these four types of yoga are stages that expand our consciousness and draw us toward wholeness, wisdom, and balance, which reach their fullest point in love, prema.

Now, since it has come to pass that the other yogas borrow kirtan from bhakti, we find that some kirtans in the spiritual marketplace offer mukti and some offer prema. The mantra chanted, your intention while chanting it, and your conceptual orientation toward the mantra determine the result of your chanting.

In part III: The Universe of Kirtan, I go into depth about the liberations and their respective types of kirtan so you can choose the tenor of yours.

Simply Chant

It takes little imagination to realize that mukti – uncovering the true self from the ancient patterns and multiple layers of false selves we've wrapped it in – is a tremendous feat. Then, to develop a spiritual body and identity and become fit to enter the spiritual world in pure love is a considerably greater achievement. Astonishingly, bhakti's method of prema-kirtan makes this higher goal comparatively easy to achieve. My spiritual master said: "Simply chant and dance!"

The difficult accomplishments of detaching from this world, developing full control of the mind and senses, gaining conclusive knowledge of the nature of Reality, removing the lifetimes of mental and emotional impressions that drive us to act in ways that sometimes even confuse us (*samskaras*), effacing the ego, and becoming single-minded in our concentration on the Supreme (*samadhi*) – all of which are the direct or indirect intentions of the other yoga methods – require absolute sense control, including celibacy. However these extraordinary attainments are automatic by-products of a bhakti practice, which also fosters in the practitioner many good qualities like humility and compassion that encompasses all beings. Though these are a natural outgrowth of bhakti, its ultimate goal is to award an eternal spiritual body and identity to the aspirant so they become fit to offer transcendental loving service to the Supreme Enchanter.

Awarding the highest attainment and doing so with comparative ease testifies to bhakti's extraordinary power – a power that accrues due to the fact that bhakti is the internal shakti, or potency, of the Supreme All-powerful.*

Of course, both the initial liberation attainable through the other yoga disciplines and the prema liberation of bhakti are lofty states, and at the moment we're consumed by everyday struggles and responsibilities. Is bhakti, then, even relevant to us where we are at the moment?

Definitely. Hearing, speaking, singing, and so on, are acts that we routinely carry out in our day-to-day lives. If the same actions are undertaken in relation to the Supreme Soul, they lead to perfection. There cannot be any spiritual practice easier than this.

Kirtan and bhakti's other practices can be done by anyone, even a child, and by culturing bhakti we experience tangible benefits in our psychophysical well-being along with the spiritual results of a yoga practice. This makes bhakti unique among all the yogas.

---

* I write at length about this special energy and Sri Radha, the goddess who embodies it, in *Bhakti Shakti: Goddess of Divine Love.*

Long-time kirtan artist Gaura Vani says, "I strongly feel that mantra is the answer to the turmoil and disconnect between people's hearts and their external lives." There's good reason to trust Gaura Vani's personal experience, as the textual foundations of bhakti indicate.

Foundations of Bhakti

The key texts for the Bhakti school are the Bhagavad Gita and the Bhagavata Purana (Srimad-Bhagavatam). These classic bhakti texts are so authoritative that followers of other paths use them to guide their own practices. In these two texts, the endorsement of kirtan is pronounced; they highlight kirtan as the primary vehicle for personal access to the divine and the perfection of life.

In the Gita, after educating Arjuna about the various types of yoga, Krishna speaks of the superiority of bhakti (Gita 6.47). Later, in the ninth chapter, Krishna underlines this point, using the words *kirtan, bhajan* (a word similar to kirtan), and *bhakti* in two sequential verses.

The ninth chapter of the Gita is titled the "Yoga of Hidden Treasure," "King of Secrets," or the "King of Knowledge." Nestled there, right in the middle of the Gita's eighteen chapters, is this secret of secrets: the highest knowledge is loving devotion. Dedication inspires the Supreme Soul to reveal himself and by knowing him everything can be known.

In that chapter, Krishna speaks of love and kirtan, as the two are intimately related. Don't we sing to and about our beloved when we're in love? Doesn't the Beloved like to hear their name sung, which in turn inspires reciprocal love?

When I first sang a song I wrote – "How I love you, how I love you, Meena" – to my granddaughter, Meena, she was just two. She nestled up against me and basked in the love song directed to her. Then with innocence, candid simplicity, and spontaneity she asked me to sing it again – and again and again.

Great souls, Krishna says, will take refuge in the divine by always chanting (*kirtayanto*) about him and offering obeisances unto him with devotion (*bhaktya*), they worship him with continuous longing for union. With their mind intent on Krishna, they love and worship him, knowing him to be imperishable and the origin of everyone.

The commonly known secret of Vedanta is that there is a unity of all things and beings. In Gita 18.63, Krishna says that knowledge of Brahman (the impersonal Oneness) is *guhya*, "confidential," but knowledge of the Lord in the heart is *guhyataram*, "more confidential," because love – reciprocal emotional exchanges between the soul and the Supreme – is the highest expression of truth.

Thus there in the Gita we learn the uncommon secret: divine love (prema) is the basis of enduring unity, capable of dissipating all disharmony. In love there is unity in the diversity because the lover and Beloved, although individuals, are one in purpose and feeling.

There's a beautiful analogy that demonstrates this point. When we're at the edge of a lake we find mental peace in perfectly placid waters; we can inhale and exhale in great calm, releasing all tension. Now if many people join us and begin throwing pebbles into different places in the water, it's disturbed, conflicted surface will create disruption to the mind. In contrast, if those same people throw their pebbles into the exact same spot, we'll find the concentric outgoing ripples pleasing, even entertaining, as their uniform appearance spreads out in the body of water. In such harmonious diversity we also experience calm.

The pebbles thrown in different places in the lake are like many people chasing after their own pleasure and self-interest. This variety is disharmonious. The pebbles thrown in the exact same place are compared to jointly serving to please the center, our Source. This diversity is pleasing and creates camaraderie and community.

The Bhagavata, the natural commentary on the Upanishads and Vedanta Sutra (known as the world's oldest wisdom texts), is considered by many Vedantins to be the final word on the entire corpus of sacred texts. It is, in fact, the final book written by the legendary Vyasa and inspired by his realized samadhi, or full absorption in the nondual Absolute. The Bhagavata is also a commentary on *omkara* and the Gayatri mantra – mantras that are said to be the first linguistic expressions and the source of the Vedas, language, and consciousness. The Gayatri mantra and omkara are two primeval sound representations of the Supreme. Indian schools of philosophy consider that understanding the Gayatri mantra and omkara is primary for unlocking transcendental knowledge and attaining liberation. The Bhagavata is a full commentary on these transcendental sounds.

And what is the Bhagavata's message? It is that beauty, affection, love, charm, and harmony are universally attractive and are our primary need. It's in truth and beauty that we find happiness and fortune. Directing us where to find that fortune, the Bhagavata repeatedly glorifies kirtan, *gita* (song), *gayan* (singing), listening to stories about the Supreme, and enacting them in plays as a means to awaken love and immerse the mind in mature contemplation and meditative absorption (dhyana and samadhi) on the Supreme. The Bhagavata further says that kirtan evokes the presence of the Divine in the heart of the chanter.

It's stated that identifying the topics a text opens and closes with is one way to determine its primary message. The Bhagavata begins and ends by enjoining the reader to engage in kirtan. Another method to determine a text's purport is to consider the points made by its speakers.

Suta is one of the main speakers in the Bhagavata, and he "builds an argument that bhakti is the real goal of human life and it is expressed through *kirtana* and its attending practices, namely, auditory reception and recollection of the instructions and stories about the Lord." (Jonathan B. Edelmann, "Kirtana in the Bhagavata Purana")

Shuka is another of the Bhagavata's primary speakers. He advises King Parikshit who, due to a curse, is preparing to die within seven days: "Constant chanting of the holy name of the Lord after the ways of the great authorities is the doubtless and fearless way of success for all, including those who are free from all material desires, those who are desirous of all material enjoyment, and also those who are self-satisfied by dint of transcendental knowledge." (2.1.11)

The Treasured, Universal Mantra
That Leads to Prema

In the sixteenth century, Sri Chaitanya Mahaprabhu galvanized the Bhakti school centered on the prema-kirtan of the Hare Krishna maha-mantra. In *Sonic Spirituality,* Steven Rosen refers to Sri Chaitanya as "the father of sacred chant as a yogic science." He brought kirtan to the public, with thousands following him, singing the Hare Krishna maha-mantra and dancing, creating a socio-spiritual revolution.

Sri Chaitanya pointed out how the Upanishads have, out of millions of sacred sounds, highlighted the sound that has the power to remove all the troubles of the current cosmic age, Kali, and resolve our own shortcomings in executing a spiritual practice. If we come to know this sound comprehensively through singing and reciting it with love, we can come to know everything. This sacred sound is the maha-mantra, or "great mantra." The mantra is "great" because it contains the power of *all* sacred mantras. The *Narada-pancaratra* declares, "All mantras and all processes for self-realization are compressed into the Hare Krishna maha-mantra."

Of special note is that no Upanishad prescribes any other mantra by which to attain mukti or prema for this current cosmic season. The *Kalisantarana Upanishad* (5–6) states:

iti sodashaka namnam
kali-kalmasha nashanam
natah parataropayah
sarva vedeshu drishyate

hare krishna hare krishna
krishna krishna hare hare
hare rama hare rama
rama rama hare hare

These sixteen names can destroy all the degrading, illusory effects of Kali. In all the Vedas, no higher or more sublime way is to be found. Hare Krishna Hare Krishna, Krishna Krishna Hare Hare, Hare Rama Hare Rama, Rama Rama Hare Hare.

Kirtan and japa of the maha-mantra, when chanted with an understanding of the mantra, is known as prema-kirtan, because it is the mantra that can awaken divine love in the heart, as exemplified in the life of Sri Chaitanya. Literally *prema-kirtan* means that kirtan which is sung by those possessed of the deepest divine love. But we can also take *prema-kirtan* to refer to the mantra kirtan that can awaken such love in us who as yet don't possess divine love.

The Bhagavata (12.3.51) states: "Although Kali-yuga is an ocean of faults, there is still one good quality about this cosmic age: Simply by chanting the holy name of Krishna, one can become free from material bondage and be promoted to the transcendental kingdom."

After 18,000 verses the Bhagavata comes to a close (12.13.23) with this message: "I offer my adoration to Hari [Krishna], the Supreme, the kirtan of whose names destroys all sins, and humble submission to whom ends sorrow and suffering."

Where Speech is Song

The Bhakti tradition explains that prema-kirtan descends from the spiritual realm with the full power of transcendental sound: *golokera prema-dhana, hari-nama-sankirtana.* The wealth of the spiritual world – its treasure – is prema, divine love, which is exported to this world through prema-kirtan, or kirtan of the Hare Krishna maha-mantra.

When we speak of what is most valuable in the spiritual realm we're speaking of inestimable, highly coveted wealth that attracts the perfectly pure-hearted people of extraordinary character and refined taste in the eternal world. We can only imagine its power to attract us who, life after life, chase after the fool's gold of fame, riches, sex, things, sensual enjoyment, and other diversions that never satiate or fully satisfy us. Spiritual wealth enriches the soul, who is by nature eternal, full of knowledge, and bliss. What is the nature then of that substance that can augment an already perfect, ecstatic existence?

Contemplating like this we can understand that divine love is not of this world and kirtan that offers it to us is not a mundane creation. It's a practice that can lift the soul to the shining regions of the pure absolute abode.

The Bhagavata validates this statement about kirtan's descent with its descriptions of many kirtans in the spiritual realm. For example, we hear of the kirtan of the young boys of Goloka, who burst into song, laughing, dancing, clapping hands, and playing on horns and flutes as they prepare to leave for an outing with Krishna to the forest. We hear the kirtan of Sri Radha who, immersed in feelings of intense separation from Krishna, speaks like a madwoman to a bumblebee. And there are descriptions of many other kirtans as well.

The *Brahma-samhita* describes that in the land of no return, "Every word is like a song." The ordinary speech of those who live in the original plane of reality is filled with metaphor, alliteration, rhyme, rhythm, double meanings, and other literary ornaments. In that realm, the residents' everyday speech flows like elegant poetry – their speech is song! With their every movement they sway gracefully – their walking is dancing! Can you imagine, then, the nature of the singing and dancing in a place where hearts are filled only with such bhakti? What kind of kirtan would that be! Our kirtan here can take us there if we practice prema-kirtan, which is the function of the soul in eternity.

Chapter 3

THE MYSTIC EAR
& HARMONY
OF THE SPHERES

*Men live on the brink
of mysteries and harmonies
into which they never enter,
and with their hands
on the door-latch
they die outside.*
– Ralph Waldo Emerson

We can make ourselves – our lives – into an exceptional and unique work of art. Kirtan can open us to our untapped potential. The divine sound vibration of kirtan can transform us in ways that psychotherapy, affirmations, visualizations, positive thinking, silent meditation, mindfulness, or hypnosis cannot. The mystery and harmony of kirtan can give you a direct, unmediated experience of the highest of attainments.

Estonian composer Arvo Pärt, who is deeply inspired by Gregorian chant, elegantly said, "The most sensitive musical instrument is the human soul. The next is the human voice. One must purify the soul until it begins to sound.... The instrument has to be in order to produce sound. One must start with that, not with the music."

Kirtan is more than just music; it's love that purifies the heart, tunes the soul, calms and clarifies the mind, releases the voice, shows a genuine way of being in the world, and offers a direct experience of the timeless, joyful self.

If you can catch the wave of sacred sound, your life will become a symphony that bathes you and others in absolute happiness. And the example you set by personal spiritual development can encourage others to leave aside selfish interests and the taking, exploiting tendency that causes all disharmony in the world and characterizes most lives. In this way, even the private kirtan you perform alone can influence the broader community and the well-being of others.

We begin the journey to where kirtan can take us by choosing what we hear. What we hear – and what we then think and speak – fashions the mind and our intuitive, cognitive, and socio-relational intelligences in the same way that food shapes the body.

Ordinary sound has astounding characteristics; sacred sound possesses wonders and shapes the spiritual self. Let's consider the nature and power of both types of sound and the attributes of our sense of hearing to help us deepen our appreciation for mantra meditation and the possibilities that await us should we take up a kirtan practice.

Sound and Mind-Body Wellness

The human ecosystem is extremely sensitive to sound. An unexpected, loud noise can make us jump, and some noises can be so intrusive that we find ourselves in fight-or-flight mode. Prolonged exposure to constant traffic noise, loud music, or any other inescapable sound can cause stress, high blood pressure, heart disease, and sleep disturbances. On the other side, listening to delta sound waves can induce deep sleep, and there's an increasing use of sound therapy to successfully (if temporarily) calm overly active nervous systems suffering from the constant assault of the unreasonable demands of modern living. Sound baths, which use gongs, quartz crystal bowls, tuning forks, and tinkling chimes, promote deep relaxation and alpha and theta brain states. They've become so popular you can design a destination vacation around them.

Sounds affect us psychologically in other ways too. Perhaps you've experienced how the inner sound of your negative thoughts or the negativity of another's words can result in physical, emotional, and spiritual illnesses. Birdsong makes people feel safe and relaxed, as do the sounds of light rain, babbling brooks, ocean waves, wind blowing through trees, and other sounds from nature. The sound of laughter can amuse us; the sound of a lion roaring can create fear. And we've all used music to uplift our spirits, or to calm or energize ourselves or change our mood in some other way.

Sounds affect us cognitively. We can't understand what's being said when two people speak at once. Based on this idea, Dr. Lloyd Glauberman, master of the dual induction technique of hypnosis, created a series of programs where he tells a separate story into each ear of the listener. This overloads the conscious mind and puts listeners into a deeply relaxed state. They are then able to make subconscious shifts in attitude due to subtle suggestions embedded in Glauberman's stories. Studies have shown that background noise above 75 dBA affects our ability to pay attention and think. Hearing classical music can improve spatial reasoning. Sound affects our perception of depth, speed, and motion. In some studies, familiar musical pieces from Alzheimer patients' youths "awakens" them.

Our bodies are resonant structures, and we swim in an ocean of sound. But human bodies aren't the only forms sound impacts. Masaru Emoto's amazing photos of the crystals that formed in frozen water samples after repeating verbal messages are striking. Saying "thank you" created a beautiful star-shaped crystal. Saying "love" created an exquisite jewel shape. A Mozart symphony created an attractive symmetrical pattern; heavy metal music created dissonant-looking crystals like ones found in water from unhealthy or dying rivers.

And we have the research of Dr. S. K. Bose and others reported in *The Secret Life of Plants* documenting ways plants and trees responded to music. The influence of certain music increased the yield of trees; plants grew toward certain music played and away from others; some music caused plants to wither and die.

My friend Akhandadhi Das relates how he conducted his own experiment. He cooked a pot of rice and divided it into two equal portions, naming one "Thanks" and the other "Fool." Every day for a week, for one minute per session, he told the rice container labeled "Thanks" how appreciative he was of the rice for feeding his family, how good it was, etc. To the rice labeled "Fool" he deprecated with unkind, hateful words spoken loudly. After a week he placed "Thanks" and "Fool" in the fridge, pulling them out nine months later. The "Thanks" rice maintained its whole-grain structure and looked fairly good; the "Fool" portion had molded and was decomposing into a liquid. After eight *years* the individual grains of the "Thanks" rice were still visible, while the "Fool" rice was a dark, disgusting, smelly liquid.

Take a minute to imagine what damage we do to our cells when we think or speak negatively, especially over a long time! Of course, many people are already aware of the power of affirmations to make positive psychological and physical shifts. But Akhandadhi's experiment tangibly shows the force of intention within sound, even on something apparently inert.

Capacities of Ordinary Sound

Sound creates form. A rudimentary example of this is seen in cymatics, the study of wave phenomena, which shows the inherent organizing principle of sound. In the 1960s, using audible sound frequencies to animate inert powders, pastes, dust, and liquids, Hans Jenny showed that the forms sound created were immensely similar to the geometric patterns found in flowers, plants, animals, and mandalas.

Sound can, with correct vibration and energy (or frequency), break glass or be used as a weapon to disorient or incapacitate a person. Scientists have developed an acoustic device to separate tumor cells from blood cells. Engineers have extinguished fire using sound waves. High-frequency sound waves can penetrate the body to produce legible images of hearts, livers, bladders, kidneys, and babies in the womb.

In *The Yoga of Sound,* Russill Paul writes, "Even the destructive capacity of sound can be put to productive use, as in the case of the lithotripter, a medical machine developed in Germany that can dissolve gallstones and kidney stones without surgery by bombarding them with sound waves. This capacity of sound to dissolve obstructions in our body and mind is one of the key principles on which the Yoga of Sound is based."

At RMIT University in Australia, scientists are testing high-frequency sound waves, inaudible to the human ear, in a myriad of applications, from building advanced materials to nanoscopic drug delivery. They have found that sound energy, with wavelengths of hundreds of micrometers, can manipulate entities like atoms or molecules which are almost a million times smaller. Distinguished Professor Leslie Yeo marvels, "It's like driving a truck into some Lego bricks and seeing them stack up neatly."

This is an example of the profound organizing capacity of sound and confirms the elementary indications we received from cymatics about the nature of sound and its ability to create form. Cymatics shows that sound can create form in inert powders and liquids; the RMIT study demonstrates that sound can create form at the level of the building blocks of matter.

Therefore, sound creates form *and* structure.

As we learn more about the quantum nature of our world, it has become undeniable that the "music of the spheres" is not just a controversial theory held by Pythagoras and other philosophers. "Quarks and electrons are musical notes on a vibrating string," says Michio Kaku, an American theoretical physicist, adding, "In essence, physics is the laws of harmony that you can write on vibrating strings. Chemistry is the melodies played on vibrating strings. The universe is a symphony of vibrating strings."

The natural order of the universe is present as vibration and information. Sound creates form – tangible, touchable, physical form. Sound has so much power! The Western mind is just beginning to explore this truth; there is much more to uncover.

Harmonies in Nature

The universe tends toward harmony. Think of the visible regularities in form in the natural world such as the patterns on zebras, tigers, lizards, and snake skins. There's the symmetry in flower petals, shells, ferns, bamboo, crystals, snowflakes, the equal growth of tree branches from the trunk, or the branching veins of a leaf. We find harmony in the flow patterns of water cutting through canyons, or the patterns created by wind in deserts. Throughout nature, we find harmonies everywhere, from the grand to the small.

Most of us are happiest when there's harmony in our relationships, minds, and bodies. Much thought goes into the design and shape of our homes and office buildings. Some of us are so sensitive to harmonies in our interior space that we employ the spatial geometry principles of feng shui or vastu to promote general well-being. Graphic design for the web, books, and advertising in all forms of media relies on harmonies of color, proportion, and type. Other art forms, too, draw on symmetry of colors, shapes, and patterns. Think of pottery, sculpture, paintings, the design of our furniture and interior decor, or even how we present a special meal on the table.

And, of course, we have harmony in music. For many of us, harmony means music, and we often use the two words interchangeably. Interestingly, when we discuss design, art, and beauty, we use other words pertaining to music, like *rhythm, congruity, balance, melody,* and *pleasing structure* to convey the "feeling" of what we want to create or identify in our environment. It's as if we're trying to translate the feeling we experience from sound into sight and form. This speaks to our experience: sound contains feeling, emotion. This is why we use "sound" words to convey feeling.

Infused with Intelligence and Feeling

We've come to understand that what we see as solid and unchanging – a table or a brick or a highway – is actually oscillating fields of pulsation: packets of information and energy. These "oscillating fields of pulsation" are sound vibration. Therefore sound contains information and energy. Put differently, sound is infused with intelligence. It is also infused with emotion. Consider how music has information *and* feeling; math underlies music. Sound is rich with information and emotion and is the vibration at the substratum of existence.

The relationship between math (knowledge, science, and logic) and music (harmony and emotion) is thought-provoking. Isn't it fascinating that Saraswati is the goddess of both learning *and* music? What is the relationship between learning and music; knowledge and feeling?

These questions are especially interesting when we consider them in relationship to kirtan and what is transmitted through mantra from the spiritual realm to us in the material sphere. Mantra invests us with transcendental knowledge and feeling from a different plane – a place with attributes and contributions we can access only through mantra meditation. Mantra meditation potently and thoroughly transform us by putting us in direct contact with transcendent knowing and feeling.

"Musical models are able to enshrine the knowledge of the universe in a very compact form," Katharine Le Mée writes in *Chant,* "It is not simply 'information,' a mere abstraction of Reality, but a participatory, active knowledge reflecting the inner nature of things and revealing itself only through the performance of song."

Ears to Hear Feeling

Consider the unique features of our ears to perceive knowledge and emotion, to sense reason and feeling within the sound vibrations we hear.

We perceive sound with the ear – the sense that rules the universe of tone, or emotion. Hearing can bring on deeper feeling states than those aroused by the eye, nose, tongue, or touch because the sense of hearing connects experientially with the heart.

In addition to the subtleties of emotions, the ear also has the uncanny ability to perceive numerical quantity in music and sounds – even subtle distinctions. In other words, the ear can perceive inherent subtle information as well as feeling and harmony.

Hans Kayser, who developed the theory of harmonics, showed that the ear can perceive numerical proportions. We can hear the difference in frequency between octaves and discern the relationships between any two notes. Every tone is a number and has an emotional quality, and the ear can hear both.

In *Nada Brahma,* Joachim-Ernst Berendt writes, "Experiments have shown that no other sense can register impulses as minimal as those that the ear can register. The amplitude of the vibrations of our eardrum lies in the area of 10^{-9}. That is smaller than the wavelength of visible light and even less than the diameter of a hydrogen atom. The smallest stimuli our ear can just barely perceive, on the other hand, have to be amplified by a factor of 10^6 in order to reach the level of the highest volume perceivable, by a factor in the million range. Were we to amplify the smallest impulses our eyes can register by the same factor, we would be blinded instantly."

Hermann von Helmholtz supports Berendt's statement *In Sensations of Tone:* "It is known that when two pendulums strike next to each other, the ear can detect down to approximately 1/200 of a second whether their strikes are simultaneous or not. The eye goes wrong at 1/24 of a second, or sometimes more, when trying to decide whether two light flashes are simultaneous or not."

With seeming fascination, Berendt probes, "Why are the data we receive from our ears so much more precise than that from our eyes? Why is the range of what we can hear so much wider – by exactly tenfold – than the range of what we can see? What is that meant to signal to us?... In addition to their measuring ability, there is their ability to sense. The most wonderful thing is how these two faculties are coupled together. In fact, it seems that in this coupling lies the greatest capacity of our ears: the ability to transfer, with unbelievable precision, material quantities into sense perceptions, conscious into subconscious, measurable things into unmeasurable ones, abstract concepts into matters of soul."

The ear is the sense that allows us access to the subtle realm of spirit through sound impregnated with knowledge (information) and devotion (feeling). *Sound is the method used by the Absolute to communicate with us.*

Our ears are the first sense to develop in the womb, and the sense of hearing is the first sense we use to interact with the outside world: we begin to hear before we're born, starting with our mother's heartbeat and, later, sounds outside her womb. Hearing remains active during deep sleep, when sound will rouse us. Hearing is also the last sense to leave us when we're dying. Our ears serve us throughout life, and they serve us well.

Sacred Sound; Sacred Geography

For these reasons it's not unreasonable to entertain the idea of the power of sacred sound. For millennia India's sages, saints, and seers have used sound technologies – mantras and meditation with mantras – to calm the mind, expand consciousness, liberate themselves from the confines of the mundane world, and find freedom from suffering by entering the finer world of spirit.

Material sound and its capacities, the yogic texts describe, are a dim reflection of spiritual sound. Sacred sound is the source of mundane sound's music, harmony, beauty, emotion, and knowledge. Therefore, spiritual sound is more capable of holding information and feeling than material sound and carries specialized information unperceivable by our senses which communicates to the soul. Sacred sound informs us with richer content and depth.

Vedanta is unambiguous about the primacy of sound and gives a comprehensive account of how sound vibration manifests the physical world of matter. Sound is also foundational to the spiritual world. When we open our ears to kirtan from that original plane of existence, we can become liberated (*anavrittih shabdat*), because that sound is brimming with the unsurpassed potency of the Absolute. The Supreme, we learn, chooses to disclose itself through the power of divine sound.

Mantras are extolled throughout the Vedic texts, and their use developed into a science. Like everything in the world of consciousness, mantras are living; they're imbued with shakti, or power. These sound formulas work internally, changing our inner tendencies and impressions and opening our awareness to different levels of reality.

We may not immediately perceive the effect of a sacred chant, but through consistent use we will experience the mantra's power to award us vision and a first-hand experience of spirit. Mantras are glasses that enable us to see the multi-dimensional world of spirit. An inflow of authentic transcendental mantras spiritualizes the senses, including the mind and intelligence, making them fit to perceive and experience spirit. Even though they are matter, the mind and intelligence can imagine and learn about the nature of spirit. But for us to actually *perceive* the spirit-self, which is categorically – ontologically – different from matter, then the senses, mind, and intelligence (which can only detect matter) must be spiritualized by an infusion of spirit by direct contact with the Supreme Purifier descending in the mantra.

This brings us to an important point to remember: the mind is different from the self. It's a limited material instrument used by the soul to function in this world. As we are not the body, we are also not the mind.

Nineteenth-century bhakti saint Bhaktivinoda Thakura writes, "From its vicinity to the soul on one side, the mind bears the character of a cognitive agency, and from its vicinity to matter on the other side, its cognitive powers are inseparably constrained to the material world. But the true and immortal man is above and inside the physical and mental bodies. Our misidentification with the material body and mind has suppressed our true nature and led us to believe the external world more than the internal."

Because the power of spiritual sound exceeds the power of material sound, spiritual sound has far more ability to calm us and bring us into harmony. The soothing sound of any instrument or musical arrangement can offer temporary physical or psychological benefit – a welcome advantage. But transcendental sound offers these physiological and psychological benefits while also uncovering the self, who is by nature secure, peaceful, joyful, and free of the pettiness, selfishness, and negative influences to which the physical and mental parts of ourselves are so prone. Spiritual sound frees the soul from its mind-body encagement and awakens it to its natural harmonious, illumined state. In that pure state all limitations and suffering tied to body and mind are resolved. Ordinary sound cannot do this.

With excellent effect, devoted prema-kirtan artist and violin virtuoso Jahnavi Harrison is mixing the ordinary sounds used in sound baths, such as those from quartz crystal bowls, with transcendental mantras, to create mantra sound baths. She demonstrates how we can creatively use mantras with other sounds and how ordinary sound can be spiritualized for increased benefit of the hearers.

Mundane sound created our predicament; sacred sound can release us. Attentively hearing the harmonies inherent in the maha-mantra in the depth of the heart makes us aware of our identity beyond the mind-body and our eternal relationship with the Original Conscious Person. By chanting the maha-mantra our previous material impressions in the mind, or *chitta,* where material impressions – our experiences and sense perceptions from this life and others – are held, are replaced with spiritual impressions of the name, form, activities, and qualities of the Supreme Person. Thus our mind, intelligence, and ego become spiritualized – ultimately, returned to their pure condition – and capable of interactions with the Personal Absolute in the world of consciousness.

In this way, the mantra communicates knowledge and feeling to us through our ears into the soul's ears. The finite's ability to touch the Infinite is first actuated through transcendental sound. The inner hearing facilitated by the external ears is our entry into sacred geography. Then we're propelled forward on our journey, and the mystical realm becomes accessible.

Harmony of Spirit

In *Systems of Vedantic Thought and Culture* (quoted in *Vaisnava Vedanta* by Mahanamabrata Brahmachari), Professor Sircar writes, "Harmony is the soul of bliss. It is because (if we see clearly) harmony helps us to feel the expanse of existence and to fathom the immensity of being. It is an indication of our fitness and capacity for feeling the vastness of existence."

We are seekers of harmony, beauty, and truth because our root source is the very form of these attributes. There are two levels of harmony: harmony of mind-body and harmony of spirit. Achieving both levels is possible when we open our hearts and fill our ears with the harmonic call of our Divine Other by chanting his holy names. Unless we achieve harmony with our Source – the reservoir of all harmony – we can't find abiding peace and joy.

This is why sound treatments and music therapies are limited in their ability to heal and satisfy us: we're not getting the full communication we need and are capable of receiving. Full harmony is possible through union with our Divine Friend. There is logic, beauty, harmony, and truth in the maha-mantra, and all of this is gradually revealed in the heart of those who chant it. The universe is a symphony of material sound; we're surrounded by it – it offers us sanctuary. This being so, now imagine the benefits of turning your attention to the superior harmonies and supreme sanctuary of the sacred sound of pre-ma-kirtan and finding for yourself a purpose-rich, peaceful life, and, finally, unearthing the highest version of your illumined self.

Chapter 4

THE PERSON IN
THE MANTRA

When the singing of the glorious qualities
of Lord Hari's personality is heard,
he enters into the hearts of men and women
to vanquish all their miseries,
as the sun dispels the darkness
and strong winds disperse the clouds.
– Bhagavata 12.12.48

Sixteenth-century bhakti saint Sanatana Goswami was an important and wealthy minister at the court of Alauddin Husain Shah when he first became enchanted by Sri Chaitanya's teachings on prema-kirtan. He later moved to the holy area of Vrindavan to immerse himself in the practice of kirtan. He became so overcome by ecstatic feelings of love in his chanting of the Hare Krishna maha-mantra that he lost all attraction to material aspirations.

Five hundred miles away, in Benares, a poor man named Jivana had spent years worshiping Shiva, hoping to get rich. One night in a dream, Shiva appeared and told him to find

Sanatana in Vrindavan. Sanatana, he said, had untold wealth and would willingly share it.

When Jivana arrived in Vrindavan he was dismayed to meet Sanatana, who was dressed in the cloth of the poor. Still, he told Sanatana about his dream. Sanatana informed Jivana that he didn't have the kind of wealth Jivana wanted, and he wondered why Shiva would have sent him to him. Then he remembered a philosopher's stone – a mystical wish-granting stone – that had long been lying in a nearby garbage pile. He told Jivana he could take that, if he liked.

Jivana eagerly searched for the stone, and when he found it, he was overjoyed. He left Vrindavan dreaming of finally becoming wealthy. But as he walked, he started to puzzle about why the stone was in the refuse pile. It occurred to him that if Sanatana cared so little for such a stone, he must have something even more valuable. What treasure could Sanatana own that made him indifferent to the philosopher's stone?

Jivana turned back and asked Sanatana. "The greatest treasure lies right here," Sanatana replied, as he placed his hand over Jivana's heart. "It is the treasure of prema for Sri Krishna. The only means of attaining this wealth is by sincere and ardent chanting of his holy names in love."

Jivana humbly petitioned Sanatana for the gift of the holy names.

Three Sacred Words of Prema-Kirtan's Maha-mantra

The maha-mantra is composed of the words *Hare, Krishna,* and *Rama.* The words of the mantra, alone or in combination, have several meanings. *Hare* means "one who removes illusion," "one who steals the mind and heart," and "one who removes the suffering of those devoted to him." *Krishna* means "he who is all-attractive." *Rama* means "he who is the source of all pleasure; the giver of pleasure; the enjoyer of all pleasures." All these are names of the Supreme Person.

Hare is an interesting word in the mantra because it's also an address to Sri Radha, the tenderhearted counterwhole of the Absolute. She is the full expression of mercy and compassion, being the personified form of Krishna's heart, and the quintessential archetype of love. As divine love personified, Sri Radha is the soul of the Supreme Soul.

It is Sri Radha who personally empowers our prema-kirtan of the Hare Krishna maha-mantra. Goddess Radha herself sings the names of her beloved Krishna, thereby showing love's natural flow to express itself by calling out to the beloved, thinking of the beloved, devoting time to the beloved.

The Mantra is Alive

The maha-mantra is the sound-body of the Supreme Person, and is therefore a vessel of pure spirit, full of knowledge and emotion. That sound-body is the Godhead in complete fullness.

The implications of the last paragraph are profound. It's a crucial fundamental truth that explains why maha-mantra meditation can affect phenomenal changes in people that enable them to make complete, lifelong transformations.

There is no difference between the maha-mantra and the Supreme Person. No difference at all. They are exactly the same. This is inconceivable to the rational (material) mind but experienced by those engaged in a mantra yoga practice. By chanting and singing the divine names one directly contacts the Supreme Person. For this reason, we find people leaving kirtans speaking about their experience of a mystical connection with the divine even though they know little or nothing about the science of mantra meditation. What is difficult or impossible to achieve in other types of yoga is easily achieved by sincere chanters; they are directly guided and supported by the Supreme.

In the Bhakti philosophy, the word *rasa* refers to a limitless ocean of loving emotion in relationship with our Divine Source.* Such rasa exists in the holy names, and those who chant with longing to be with our Divine Friend can swim in that excellent ocean. The *Padma Purana* states, "The holy name is a touchstone, is Krishna himself, and is a living personification of rasa. It is complete, supremely pure, and eternally liberated due to the nondifference between the name and the named."

Mantras bring forth immediate apprehension of the Reality they signify when we respectfully receive them from those lovingly dedicated to them. In other words, mantras are transmitted from heart to heart and, when successfully planted, award transcendental vision. The preceptor who has an established, active, loving relationship with the Name imparts the mantra into the heart. Love, or in the beginning, respect, must be present to receive the Names properly. When love, or bhakti, is absent, the person of the mantra exits the mantra (or never enters it), and what is left is ordinary sound.

So we want to hear the mantra from a realized adept who models the behavior of one infused with divine love and who

---

* We'll learn more about *rasa* and how it is the gold standard of spiritual wealth in chapter ten.

therefore can guide us in how to progress in mantra meditation. When we do, the mantra remains alive because it's rooted in a correct understanding of and approach to the mantra.

Bhaktivinoda Thakura explains that the full brilliance of the holy names can only manifest when a mantra meditation practice is oriented by *tattva,* or understanding of the true nature of the Name, the soul, the material world, the Lord, and their mutual relationships. We receive this by hearing from saintly people whose lives are informed by the sacred texts.

In commenting on the declaration in the Bhagavata (5.5.2) that "One can attain the path of liberation from material bondage only by rendering service to highly advanced spiritual personalities." A. C. Bhaktivedanta Swami writes, "The human body is like a junction. One may either take the path of liberation or the path leading to a hellish condition. How one can take these paths is described herein. On the path of liberation, one associates with *mahatmas* [liberated souls], and on the path of bondage one associates with those attached to sense gratification."

It's common knowledge that we are formed by the company we keep. Those who desire to move forward will seek out the uplifting company of those who are advanced on the path.

The Bhagavata describes a person who attempts a practice without such a teacher, or guru, to be like a merchant sailing the ocean without a helmsman. My guru said that one will fly her own plane after she's had sufficient training on the ground and in the air. That training in bhakti comes from a guru whose heart is completely captivated by bhakti.

As we need credentialed, competent teachers to become doctors and lawyers – to become proficient in anything really – we require guidance to go to the zenith of human consciousness.

We need to receive the mantra from a guru-adept who is chanting with advanced love. This inspires our own chanting practice and through that guidance we remain connected with the pure Name, Sri Nama.

Patrick Bernard, kirtan artist and author of *Music as Yoga,* writes, "To listen to and sing spiritual sound vibrations while treading in the master's footsteps constitutes the path to perfection and freedom from doubt and fear for all. This path is not only offered to students wishing to perfect their ideological research, but also to those who have already triumphed in their efforts."

Welcoming the Mantra

Mantras are independent. We don't own them, and we can't make demands of them or exploit them for our own purposes. We can use them outside the context of a yoga discipline – something many people do – but the person in the mantra will not reveal him or herself to insolent or disrespectful chanters. Nor will the secrets of the mantra be revealed to those who don't understand that the person in the mantra is real, or to those who don't welcome the person with respect, humility, and affection.

Used according to one's own whims, mantras become ordinary sounds that, when repeated, may still calm the mind simply because when the mind focuses on *anything* other than its endless loops of thoughts, it finds a little peace. But this result has little to do with spirit.

Man means "mind"; *tra* means "instrument." Hence the definition of mantra is "a sound instrument or vehicle that transports the mind," "that which protects a person meditating on it," "a transformative tool or instrument," or "an instrument enabling the mind to bring us liberation." If we choose our mantra carefully, receive it properly, and chant it with focus and dedication, the mantra will take us beyond the mind into the land of spirit – the land of love and beauty.

For mantra meditation to be effective, we should stick to one mantra and be steady in our meditation practice. If you want to get down to the water table when digging a well, you must dig down deep in the same spot. A habit of changing or inventing will not help us progress.

Because the maha-mantra and Krishna are identical, chanting the maha-mantra without offense brings us directly into Krishna's presence; we meet Sri Nama, the holy name, as an unlimited, loving, personal being. And he initiates the ability to control the mind and the inner transformation required to bring us peace and happiness. He also ushers us into the highest transcendental state of divine love and awards us a transcendental body.

Bhaktivinoda Thakura writes that the holy name is unlimited, beginningless, fully conscious, invested with all the transcendental energies of Krishna, and can award any desire.

The superior benefit of specifically chanting the holy name of Krishna – as opposed to the names of other forms of divinity – is expressed in the *Brahmanda Purana* (2.36.19): "By repeating Krishna's name just once, one attains the same benefit that accrues from thrice repeating the thousand holy names of Vishnu." Mahadeva Shiva further elaborates in the *Padma Purana:* "Liberation (mukti) is attained from the name of Rama, whereas devotion in the completion stage of divine love (prema) is attained from the name of Krishna."

We can note that by comparing Krishna's name with his expansions such as Vishnu and Rama, we're being nudged toward understanding that Krishna is the source of all forms of divinity, which is why his name has superior potency. We'll consider these points of philosophy in more depth later in chapter ten.

As the sonic avatar, or the holy name Sri Nama, the Supreme Person descends from his home to console, counsel, and accompany us onward as a personal friend. In a poetic verse the *Skanda Purana* happily proclaims,

> *madhura-madhuram etan mangalam mangalanam*
> *sakala-nigama-valli-sat-phalam chit-svarupam*
> *sakrd api parigitam sraddhaya helaya va*
> *bhrgu-vara nara matram tarayet krsna-nama*

The name of Krishna is the sweetest of the sweet, the most auspicious of the auspicious. The eternal spiritual fruit from the vine of all the Vedas delivers a human being when it is chanted even once, faithfully or negligently.

We simply chant with basic trust in the power of Sri Nama and focus our attention on the sacred sound vibration with a desire to please the person in the mantra. This lets us begin to build a foundation for pure love.

Love makes us want to see our beloved satisfied and happy. We want to spend time with a person we love; we want to care for that person. We like to serve our beloved, to nourish them with good food and comfort. We want to hear them when they speak, and we express our love for them through all our words and actions. When love is unconditional, we don't even think of our self-interest. These are natural characteristics of love.

Loving a Person We Cannot See

The nine limbs (angas) of the body of bhakti are designed to draw out from the heart expressions of love for our Divine Friend. We will develop an emotional bond with the Supreme Person by treating him as a person. But how do we interact with a person we can't see?

The ancient texts describe that the Absolute agrees to appear in forms that have been made to represent his likeness according to details described in those texts. This form is called arca-vigraha or "the form of worship." It can be a form we meditate on in the mind or presented in a piece of art – painted on canvas or carved from marble, stone, or wood. Other media have also been used throughout history. Bhaktivinoda Thakura writes, "If a word provokes a thought, a watch indicates time, and a sign tells us of history, why shouldn't a picture of the deity bring higher thoughts of and feelings for the transcendental beauty of the Divine Person?"

At home one can create a sacred space, perhaps an altar, then take a favorite picture or carving (murti) of the Divine and place it prominently on the altar. We can then offer incense, flowers, Q-tips dipped in essential oils – sweet scents – to our Friend. I like to keep a vase of fresh flowers on my altar. I've planted gardenias, honeysuckle, jasmine, roses, and moghra in my garden, and I also have a gorgeous magnolia gracing my front yard. If I had more of a green thumb, I might plant more flowers. It's an act of meditation to take a few minutes out of a hectic day to step into a garden and pick a few flowers to prepare a vase.

When a person comes to visit, we make sure to give them something to drink and if they're hungry, to feed them. You can make offerings of food before the picture or murti, serving your Divine Friend on a plate and utensils reserved for his use. Ask him to accept the meal along with the effort you took to cook it. Children love to make offerings. While you cook you can think that you're serving your Supreme Friend by cooking for him. When you plan your meals for the week and shop for your family, keep him in mind; he is the originating member of your household. When you prepare and eat vegan or vegetarian food in this way, you honor *prasada,* "mercy." This elevates our material need to eat to a spiritual activity. *Prasada* creates bhakti samskaras, devotional impressions in the mind, and purifies body and mind.

Some people I know develop more ways to respectfully and personally worship their Friend. You can meditate on placing your Friend in a comfortable bed at night and waking him in the morning, or you can give him a nice place to sit along with a cup of fresh water.

In your sacred space, you can chant the maha-mantra quietly on a set of beads made for that purpose or do kirtan. The picture or murti of the Divine is a visual aid to help you focus the mind on the object of your meditation. If you spend time chanting in your sacred space, it will become a sanctuary that warmly welcomes you to sit in prayer or contemplation or converse directly with your Divine Friend. The more you welcome him as a person through these small daily activities, the deeper the communication you'll receive from him – and the more your heart will bloom and move you closer to pure love and a transcendental destination.

The following nine limbs of bhakti may give you other ideas how to express affection for your Divine Friend.

The Body of Bhakti

The nine limbs of the "body" of bhakti are

1. Hearing (*sravanam*)
2. Chanting (*kirtanam*)
3. Remembering (*smaranam*) the names, forms, qualities, and activities of the Supreme Person
4. Offering loving service (*pada-sevanam*)
5. Respectfully worshiping (*arcanam*) the deity
6. Offering prayers (*vandanam*) (composing your own and reciting others' prayers)
7. Serving his desires in the world (*dasya*)
8. Making friends (*sakhyam*) with him
9. Surrendering everything to him (*atma-nivedanam*)

If you study these limbs you'll notice that kirtan is a principal activity in most of them. The limbs "hearing" and "remembering" stem from kirtan, and "prayer" is a form of kirtan too. Of course, "chanting" refers directly to kirtan. But "chanting" also refers to speaking about the Supreme Person. After we hear of his activities, qualities, and form, we speak about them; speaking is a powerful way to remember. Among the many activities involved in "offering loving service," "respectfully worshiping," and "serving his desires in the world," kirtan, chanting, and speaking to others about him are included. In this way, kirtan is the centerpiece of bhakti.

Our words about Krishna are especially powerful. The Bhagavata (12.12.49–50) says: "That speech alone is delightful and begets newer and newer taste, that speech alone produces an endless festival of joy for the heart, that speech alone dries up the ocean of sorrow for human beings, in which the glory of Hari [Krishna] is constantly sung." Why does speaking about the Supreme Person bring about such results? Because kirtan induces divine love for him and melts the heart. We want a heart so butter soft that it melts in supreme love, which gives us a taste of the highest ecstasy, and establishes us, finally, rejoined with the Soul of our soul in loving service.

Kirtan of the Gita and the Bhagavata

In addition to chanting the Names, bhakti meditation is enriched by learning more about the Personal Absolute through hearing from sacred texts. The person in the maha-mantra is the speaker of the Bhagavad Gita, a profound discussion on consciousness, the self, the nature of being, the makeup of the world, karma, time, and the Supreme.

The word *gita* means "song," and the Bhagavad Gita is the kirtan sung by the Primordial Person himself. Hearing it, studying it, and learning its message is also kirtan. By hearing the song of the Supreme we come to know something about him, but also about the self, who has a relationship with him. The Bhagavad Gita is a conversation between Krishna and his dear friend and confidant Arjuna, held at a moment of deep existential grief for Arjuna. Rather than solace Arjuna with platitudes, Krishna teaches him the basics of the four yoga schools with an emphasis on how to act in the world in a way that fosters both material and spiritual well-being. Through this conversation we learn about the laws of the universe that bind us as well as how to release ourselves from them. We also learn a more complete definition of knowledge and how to acquire it. By hearing the Gita we develop an appreciation, even admiration, for its speaker.

But the Gita comprises only an hour of Krishna's life when he showed himself on earth. There's much more we can know about his life in the earthly realm both before and after he spoke the Gita. He is the subject of the 18,000-verse Bhagavata, which is rich with the kirtan of Krishna's personality, qualities, psychology, activities, abode, associates, avatars, energies, and expansions. Hearing the details of the life of the Absolute makes him more relatable and thus loveable, and this nourishes our feelings for the person in the mantra.

According to the Bhagavata, the person in the mantra is full of good qualities, learned in all fields of knowledge, courageous, talented in all the arts, quick-witted, skillful, expert, beautiful, jovial, tolerant, merciful, playful, pleasing to hear, a genius, witty, grateful, the cynosure of everyone's eyes, controlled by love, and fully immersed in pure love. He is surrounded by those who love fully, and he gives himself fully in love to them. He is the all-attractive person. It is enjoyable to hear about him – and in his form as Sri Nama, he is easily approached.

There are numerous histories in the Bhagavata of Krishna's charming activities, and we can choose any of them to contemplate and meditate on. The expansive, loving nature of the person Krishna, and the details of his activities, have inspired artists for millennia, and we have a wealth of paintings, sculptures, poems, dramas, dance, and other literary works, and other expressions of love and appreciation for him. The Gita and Bhagavata continue to inspire creativity in hearts around the world.

And both texts are important works of knowledge to fortify the intelligence and create an illuminated bedrock on which to walk forward with confident, secure steps on the inner journey. Knowledge inspires trust in the process, which propels us onward with determination, enthusiasm, and steadiness.

From these books we receive content for our meditation. In other words, we can fill the mind with meditation-worthy images. Adding details of Krishna's activities, qualities, and relationships into our consciousness spiritualizes the mind. We know how powerful images and stories are from TV, movies, social media, video games, ads, art, books, and other media. Things we hear and see can stay with us for decades, like well-crafted ads or jingles we can't seem to shake. That's because we *feel* the stories we see and hear, and we remember what we feel. What we feel becomes alive within us.

The problem is stories and scenes felt from the temporal world keep us bound because they strengthen our identification with the temporal – the material body, mind, and the imagined false self. When we focus on content that is spiritual, especially in the form of the stories about and qualities of the Supreme, along with the expressions in media of his forms and expansions that we find attractive, we uproot the material samskaras, the ancient impressions we've etched onto our mental body, and replace them with impressions that liberate us from all untruth and repeated birth and death.

Bhakti is the only yoga that offers the dual benefit of simultaneously removing material samskaras and creating spiritual ones that take the atma toward liberation. These new impressions begin to create a spiritual body and identity – something that develops to its fullest in the mature stage of a bhakti practice.

All of these uncommon gifts easily come to us through prema-kirtan, like a succulent fruit that drops from a tree into our open palm as soon as we extend a hand.

Part II

The Experience of Kirtan

Chapter 5

THE YOGA
OF KIRTAN

In this age of quarrel and hypocrisy,
the only means of deliverance
is the chanting of the holy names
of the Lord. There is no other way.
There is no other way. There is no other way.
– Brihan-naradiya Purana 3.8.126

When we sing the holy names, we'll find at first that we can experience a little of the natural spiritual emotions the self has for the Supreme. Although we want to repeatedly feel these coveted emotions, they are not yet developed enough, and so they remain largely inactive in the heart.

But a regular mantra meditation practice calls up these treasured feelings from the innermost chambers of our heart and give us an opportunity to be with them more often and for longer periods of time. The more we practice hearing and chanting, the more the feelings become activated. The more prevalent they become in us, the deeper they develop. We can then draw from them the inspiration and determination to transform ourselves. We think, "This is so beautiful, so real, so deep. I want more. I want to dive deep."

Of his experience in musical kirtan Jai Uttal writes, "Although the practice itself is simple, the internal process that it stimulates is vast and mysterious. Externally, we're just singing repetitive songs with simple melodies and a few Sanskrit words. We try to put our analytical minds to the side and sing from the heart. We try to channel whatever emotion we're feeling into the song. Then the magic happens: Walls constructed long ago come crumbling down. Wounds that we never knew were there begin to heal. Long-submerged emotions come to the surface. As we sing, we immerse ourselves in an endless river of prayer that has been flowing since the birth of the first human beings. And somehow, effortlessly, we move into a meditative state that creates a safe haven for the flower of the heart to unfold."

Beyond the Music

Those who are new to kirtan often don't realize that kirtan is not a musical genre. Rather it is a transmusical meditation, an activity that has descended from beyond this world of limitation and death to give life to the souls trapped here. Kirtan is a function of the soul, not the voice. It's an expression of the heart – voice and instruments are meant to support the heart's flowering. And kirtan can be done without instruments. Kirtan is not the singular domain of musicians and vocalists; it's not a competition of who has the best voice or who can play the drum with the most expertise – though sometimes we witness this misunderstanding in public kirtans.

If we feel we lack musical talent or even doubt our voice, we may think it's safer to attend only public kirtans where we can meld into the group instead of singing kirtan alone, at home. But it's in the comfort of our own home, on our own schedule, where a kirtan practice is easiest. The wonder of kirtan and private japa meditation of the maha-mantra is meant to be brought into our lives daily, and chanting and singing alone, at home, is a good way to actually find one's voice and the depth of one's prayer.

That said, public kirtans are certainly special. Around Thanksgiving every year there's an event called Festival of the Holy Name. Though I do japa and kirtan daily, I look forward to the event all year long. Every evening for a week leading up to Thanksgiving weekend, there's a three-hour evening kirtan. Then on Friday and Saturday, kirtans are held without break from 9:00 A.M. to midnight. I sit (and dance!) for the entire two days without distraction, surrounded by hundreds of devoted kirtan singers, who are also submerging themselves in the waves of ecstatic emotions the holy names evoke.

Before we sit to chant, we know we're not chanting to escape or "get lost" in the experience; we're here to find ourselves and our relationship with the Supreme. We want to please him. Therefore we invest ourselves and carefully, completely, give our attention with the intention to sing for the pleasure of the Eternal Divine Person.

The melodies, the glorious sound of the instruments, and the beautiful voices of my fellow chanters come together to shape a fun, easy way to meditate. But these are externals. The melody, voices, and instruments are to assist us in stilling the mind so we can turn inward. The purpose of kirtan is to hear the mantra; to spend time with the mantra; to welcome the mantra as a friend, to give pleasure to the Supreme Person. By engaging with kirtan as a yoga practice, we are given many gifts.

There's something extraordinary when you experience a profound moment of inner connection or overwhelming pure love, open your eyes and see a friend riding the height of the same wave, and you exchange heartfelt smiles that are more knowing and more gratifying than any sensual experience because this exchange transcends the mind-body. These moments of communing with the Supreme and feeling his presence accumulate hour by hour, sending chanters soaring into delight. Without fail, I gain realizations about the holy names, have a direct experience of Krishna's presence, or see ways I can improve myself. Inevitably, I leave with renewed determination for my private daily practice and a joy that carries me for months.

The Inner Journey with Japa

Then the next day, I return to my quiet japa meditation, beginning before the sun rises. I enter my sacred room, a place free of distraction, as I have done for nearly fifty years, pick up my japa mala (rosary beads), and begin chanting the maha-mantra with a prayer: "Please accept me. Please engage me. Please remove the obstacles that keep me from serving you with love."

Every day is different. Sometimes I come to my meditation with a peaceful mind and focusing on the sound vibration is relatively easy. Other days, when I sit, my mind is disturbed about the behavior of a friend or family member, or some lacking in myself, or I'm thinking too much of responsibilities that I must tend to. Some days I'm tired, others alert. Some days I feel resistance to my practice, others I submerge in profound happiness.

In all circumstances, however, I come to the chanting with the same intention: today my mind and I will work cooperatively to achieve a spiritual goal. We're going to hear the holy names. Sometimes miracles occur. Often they don't. Some days it seems I didn't hear a single repetition of the name, but these days are now infrequent. What's important is that I dedicatedly, determinedly, take the inner journey every single day. This has a cumulative effect that is nothing short of amazing. I have spoken with many dedicated chanters about this. Each person's journey is unique to their intention, effort, and desire. Yours will be novel and inspiring and gratifying beyond your imagination – as I've experienced myself, and as confirmed by the many chanters with whom I've spoken.

It is in the familiar quiet of cultivating my inner landscape that I'm relieved of the turmoil of the mind and senses and given resources to turn fear into fearlessness, attachment into detachment, to find deep prayer, and to accept loss and grief and release them both. I lose the need to solve problems and control situations and learn to navigate, cope, and transcend life as it unfolds.

From years of experience, I rest calm in the knowing that the petty, seemingly large material problems are resolved in due course and my practice guides me through them. I remain confident that what I don't know but need to know will be revealed. Chanting has changed the way I perceive life. I no longer thirst for material things. What I hated or disliked no longer disturbs me; or if it sometimes does, I find these thoughts easily released before they even form a full sentence. Bothersome exchanges in relationships don't hold the same charge. What was once negative or annoying no longer troubles me. The whole world looks different, sounds different, and feels different.

What have I discovered? These shifts come from an adjustment of my inner world brought about by my practice and bring peace and calm. This isn't an artificial or temporary imposition on my mind. The desires that once harassed me really have quieted; I now desire only prema. I understand that everyone and everything around me has a connection with the Supreme. As the years pass, so many material things have less and less importance.

I know that I was lifted to great heights during group kirtan at the Festival of the Holy Name because I carefully nourish a bond of love with Sri Nama every day.

All of this and more is granted to one who takes up a practice.

A Japa Practice

Here's the fulcrum of the entire practice: whenever and wherever the mind wanders, bring it back to the sound of the Names. This is kirtan yoga: hear the sacred sound. That's it. Hear. Listen. Become receptive. Become a receptacle.

Make a little space in your heart and give time to chanting; both the mantra and the practice will become a treasure and, as conscious listeners, we'll gradually perceive more and more of what the Supreme Person is trying to say to us. In *Music as Yoga*, Patrick Bernard writes, "For listening, it should be recalled, is primarily opening one's heart, or according to [Alfred] Tomatis, 'entering into understanding and loving communion with another being.' "

This is the type of hearing we are to cultivate in our meditation on the holy names. We are opening our hearts. We are becoming molded into a vessel of love by hearing the names of Love Personified.

As I chant, I become aware that I need to improve myself, and I open myself to being shown ways I can grow. Sometimes I ask to be shown what one thing I can do today to shift into a spiritual awareness and transformational activity. I have understood the temporary, suffering nature of the world, and I've heard about the nature of the spiritual world by hearing daily from sacred texts. I also remember that I'm a spiritual being, a spark of spirit. All this is in the background of my awareness; it causes feelings to arise because I sense how dependent I am on mercy and how much kindness I've received. I cannot conquer or control. I require mercy. Therefore my chanting becomes like a cry. My spiritual master said to cry like a child crying for its mother. If I'm lucky I may be able to cry.

When I chant, I try to leave aside all temporal concerns, my likes and dislikes, my desires or things I hate, my senses of urgency or complacency, and any pain I may feel in my body, by focusing all my attention on the sound of the names, which seem to play in my heart. The sound enters my ears and goes straight to the heart. Sometimes I even place my left hand on my heart and feel the mantra there as I try to raise feeling for the Supreme Person.

As I continue chanting, perception shifts. At times I lose awareness of the beads, my body, breath, time, or where I'm sitting. I'm not trying to settle into meditation, I'm already immersed. I've regularly heard about the power of the Name before I come to sit and meditate. I've experienced the power of the Name before, and I pray that Sri Nama will be present with me. I've repeatedly heard about Krishna's form, names, qualities, and activities, and sometimes a perception of his qualities or a darshan (vision) of one of his activities impresses itself on my mind. I have made deposits into my consciousness through hearing. Now some of the auspicious content rises naturally in the mind, without effort. I observe what rises, but I keep my focus on hearing.

Japa meditation can be practiced for fifteen minutes or two hours or more, as we have time and inclination. Repeat the mantra at a comfortable pace, with your mind focused on the sound. If it helps, look at a picture of Radha and Krishna (or your treasured form of the Supreme Person) or the words of the mantra written on paper. Chanting engages three senses – the ears, the tongue, and the sense of touch as you move the beads; using a visual aid of some sort adds the eyes to this list. In this way, japa is a friendly way to control the mind and meditate.

Expect your mind to wander. The mind will go off task repeatedly. But there's nothing more essential to the practice of japa or kirtan than to focus the mind on the sound of the names.

I can tell you from my own experience that if you don't train the mind right from the beginning, you'll develop poor mental habits that will make it harder for you to chant long-term. It's best to train your mind as soon as you begin mantra meditation. Don't let it veer from the sound of the mantra. Whenever it inevitably does leave the mantra, gently bring it back to the sound of your chanting.

If you are strict with the mind, it will learn that you're serious and not going to let up. It'll still behave in ways that require your exertion to control it, but it will give up more and more often. If you don't let it slide – even for a moment – not only will your meditation improve, but you'll also remain more in control, and that ability to control your mind will be useful to you in other activities.

Do you ever find yourself feeling compelled to do something unbeneficial that you actually don't want to act on? Would you find it helpful to control what you think about others or, and perhaps especially, what you (accidentally) say to them? Do you think that an ability to really focus your mind would help you at work, school, or completing other tasks? There are many ways learning to control the mind will benefit you and getting the mind's cooperation during mantra meditation is an excellent, powerful place to begin the process.

There may be times when you have to be very strong and demanding with the mind, and other times when you need to take a firm, yet gentle approach. You'll find your own way into cooperation – it's simply part of the work of a spiritual practice to train the mind and bring it back from its wanderings. Take it over and over by the hand, like an errant child, and return it to concentrating on the sacred sound of the mantra.

Your efforts will be rewarded. If you learn to focus on sacred sound, you'll get the ultimate spiritual benefits of the mantra and also experience the multiple side benefits of meditation – you'll be able to release stress, decrease anxiety, tame anger, sleep better, be kinder, feel happier, enhance your memory, and reset your nervous system.

As valid as all these tips are about controlling the mind, you'll learn that the mind will follow the heart. Try to bring some feeling for the Supreme Person into your chanting and your mind will more easily align with your higher self. Feeling can be aroused by hearing about the person. In the next chapter we'll hear about how to become single-hearted and thereby improve our feeling approach to mantra meditation.

Trust the Process

Meditation is a process – a profound process of positive inner change that will derail the karmic trajectory you've been on for lifetimes. Such a transformation will bring you into your true self and home.

Simply turn yourself over completely to the maha-mantra, relaxing into full surrender, hearing the mantra and allowing the Protector and Friend in the mantra to guide you.

Luckily, meditation on the maha-mantra doesn't require advanced knowledge of kundalini, akashic records, the five *koshas* (sheaths), the 72,000 *nadis* and *marma* points (the body's energy channels), or the seven chakras and how to balance them. You don't need to hide out in a cave to meditate, focus the eyes on the tip of the nose as the Gita and many yoga texts prescribe, or raise your life airs to the crown chakra. You don't need to know Sanskrit vowels and consonants and how each is associated with a different part of your body, resonating with your left cheek or your forehead or your right abdomen or your plasma. You don't need to learn how the body is a blueprint of nature and how to activate your eyes. You don't need to take time to learn rituals or *mudras* (hand gestures), how to balance the energies of the planets or remove mental *vrittis* (thoughts stemming from karmic impressions). It's okay if you don't know all the asanas or never try pranayama. Don't worry if you don't understand the three *gunas,* the five gross material elements (earth, water, air, fire, and ether), or three subtle material elements (mind, intelligence, and ego). You don't have to know the science of chanting Sanskrit meters. You don't have to intone or time the mantras perfectly according to ritual or tradition. None of these knowledge systems or activities are spiritual in themselves and therefore they cannot help you transcend matter. What's important to master in other practices is not a requisite here. The holy names award all the benefits of any other system and more.

What would be good, however, is to learn to pronounce the mantra you're chanting correctly – the work of a minute. I've made a recording (see the QR code at the beginning of the appendixes to take you to the recording). Beyond that, your other tasks are simply to sit in a way conducive to paying attention and to listen. That's it. From there Sri Nama will work his magic on your psychophysical body and reveal knowledge of himself, yourself, and the spiritual realm as you develop your ability to hear the sacred.

Although everything possibly available to the soul is attainable through this mantra, for your ultimate benefit it's best not to ask for material boons. All knowledge is contained in the maha-mantra and revealed in the heart of a practitioner in the course of an earnest practice. Everything is accomplished simply by giving yourself to hearing, to sincerely chanting Sri Nama, to trying to please Krishna.

In *Bhakti Yoga,* Edwin Bryant writes, "Hence, in addition to its bliss-bestowing potential, *kirtana* is especially effective in removing impure influences from the mind (the *kleshas*).... Other purificatory processes may eliminate the negative *karmic* consequences of unrighteous action, but they do not eradicate the initial impulses or desires, called *samskaras* in yoga psychology, that prompted such behavior in the first place. Hence, those *samskaras* (not to be confused with *samsara*) can activate again. This is sometimes compared with an elephant taking a bath in the river only to emerge from the water and then roll in the sand again. *Kirtana* eradicates the *samskaras* themselves, not just their *karmic* consequences, and hence is considered the supreme purifier."

As you meditate daily with Sri Nama you will develop more of an attraction to and enjoyment of the chanting. Your own inner spiritual wisdom will begin to unfurl, letting you step forward onto the path of devotion, and as you take those steps toward the Supreme, he will hurry forward toward you if you stay with the practice.

I end my days by reading a bhakti text and sometimes sing another kirtan. Reading sacred texts strengthens the intelligence with logic, spiritual truths, and philosophy that corrects our vision and fortifies our determination to embrace a daily yogic practice and lifestyle. These texts also explain the meaning and potency of the Names, which inspires our mantra meditation japa and kirtan, gives us reason to proceed, and informs us where we are on the path, what to avoid, and what to include. And they otherwise act as a compass to guide us through the jungle of uncertainty created by our minds and our lives.

Private Kirtan

In addition to private japa meditation, you can also practice private kirtan. If you don't have or play a musical instrument, you can clap your hands or get some finger cymbals. Otherwise, simply sing your heart out. It makes no difference if you're on tune or in beat; what matters is that you sing the Names with love. Center yourself in the heart and sing the mantra with whatever affection you can find there. The love will increase by this practice, and as you progress in your ability to focus on hearing and chanting, the more you can dip into feeling – and the more these cherished feelings will develop when you practice, maturing over time. As your love for the Supreme increases, you'll begin to feel separation from your Beloved. We want to come to the point of feeling so much separation that we cry. Krishna responds to this genuine feeling. When we can cry for the Supreme Person, we can know that we're making good progress – in the language of the bhakti poets, we can know that the heart is melting and becoming pure.

There are hundreds of melodies that can be used for chanting the maha-mantra, and you can mine tunes on YouTube or other internet or music channels, where you'll find many maha-mantra kirtans. Many of the tunes are simple to learn – though there are as many that are complex. Just find some you like and learn them. I've gathered a few kirtans to accompany this book. (See the QR code at the beginning of the appendixes.)

I have a harmonium and a mridanga drum and know how to use both in very basic ways. Though I have no real musical talent, I've often experienced the same intensity of connection and affection while singing alone as I do in a group – sometimes more. I sit in front of my harmonium and play one of the tunes there are for the maha-mantra, and simply sing to my picture of Radha and Krishna. I think of serenading them. If you like, you can add other elements to your practice if they inspire your meditation and thereby help you express feeling. A friend of mine always lights incense and candles before singing, and openly states her intention before chanting.

To be honest, even kirtan events like Festival of the Holy Name cannot replace the intimacy and fulfillment of my treasured private meditations, which have deepened through years of practice. Nothing can replace or duplicate the time you take with yourself daily to leave the external world and connect with that which is transcendent to time, space, and karma – the translocal place, where the self actually resides. It's an event that through repetition over time creates strength, flexibility, ability to discern matter from spirit, a willingness to heed the call of spirit, and direct experience of the vast universe beyond the mind and senses.

This is the transsensual process by which the sight of the self is developed and the self can see the self. This is the process

Krishna established whereby one becomes qualified to see him directly. There is no experience in the world that matches it or is worthy of effort, by comparison.

Grow in the Gaps

Let's greedily gather all the available moments not swallowed by work, sleep, and responsibilities to our families and communities for mantra meditation. After all, we're trying to unravel untold lifetimes of habits and break the beginningless cycle of karma. So little time is left for this most important activity.

After my morning japa meditation, I continue to fit the mantra into all the little nooks and crannies of my life. When I'm not singing a tune or listening to a recorded kirtan, I chant the maha-mantra – sometimes under my breath – or listen to classes or audio books while I shower, dress, drive, shop, walk, cook, exercise, do asanas and pranayama, or clean. I chant quietly while I wait in line somewhere or while I'm on hold on the phone, while I walk from my car into the grocery store, while I'm in bed with an illness, and as I'm falling asleep. I feel elated when my yoga practice is so absorbing that I chant in my sleep because this is evidence that the mantra is penetrating deep into my heart.

Think about the all the times that are otherwise filled by mental chatter. Fill those instead with the holy names and give those moments meaning and purpose: commit to grow in the gaps.

Let's now consider the inner work that runs parallel to chanting the mantra.

Chapter 6

HEALING
THE HEART

The true inner self must be drawn up
like a jewel from the bottom of the sea,
rescued from confusion, from indistinction,
from immersion in the common,
the nondescript, the trivial, the sordid, the evanescent.
– Thomas Merton

You can uncover your true, radiant nature, spread light in the world, and reduce the confusion in which the world is drowning. You can become a spiritual luminary; it's an achievement possible for any human being. The world needs that version of you desperately.

Chanting the mantra is a powerful, direct, and gentle way to efface the false ego, an absolute requirement to set the real self free. The false ego and its desires are our primary impediments to self-truth and lasting happiness. Why not dismiss the false self now? After all, it's on death row anyway: when this body dies our current sense of self expires too.

How can we experience spirit while remaining convinced

that we're the material body-mind? We require more than theoretical knowledge to understand the difference between the spirit-self and the body-mind; we need realized knowledge that can be lived. And that requires cleansing the heart of the ignorant mental impressions of untold lifetimes; we need to see with the eyes of the soul.

A Little Help from our Friend

An important and compelling insight Vedanta offers is that we must distinguish the self from the mental body; the mind is the culprit keeping us bound – it's not our friend. When you fully acknowledge your predicament, you can find the clarity and determination to begin your spiritual journey in earnest. Then you make an interesting discovery: to achieve freedom from repeated deaths of a physical body (liberation), you must die many deaths of the mental body in this life (ego effacement). The more one gives up the subtle body, or the false ego, the closer one comes to self-realization.

Dying those many deaths of ego effacement doesn't mean erasing the mind. Rather, dying to the mental body means pulling off all the masks, the foreign coverings, the layers of predispositions, misconceptions, misidentifications, and all the many qualities that don't serve us well, such as hypocrisy, greed, envy, arrogance, dishonesty, and resistance. We must pull away the various social selves – the familial, the career, the political selves. *All* transitory selves have to be dismantled. We thought these our friends, but they are enemies of self-truth.

That's quite a list, I know, and it contains much psychological and spiritual work. It points to the fact that our hearts require a major realignment. When you chant the Names, they'll find and remove ignorant material impressions and, simultaneously, establish illuminating spiritual insights that you begin to perceive. Through each step of this process, the person in the mantra personally helps you.

B. R. Sridhar Swami says, "Krishna, who is situated in the heart of the devotee, strikes at the root of all the material urges that infect his heart, reducing them to oblivion. When the devotee brings Krishna, the Soul of all souls, into his heart, no evil can remain there. Swiftly is the hard knot of mundane ego severed, all doubts are slashed, and all mundane action is exhausted from the earnestly aspiring chanter."

Of all the yogas, bhakti offers the easiest way of ego effacement. The Bhagavata (3.25.33) says, "As the fire of digestion easily digests consumed food, so the cultivation of bhakti quickly destroys the subtle body [the impurities of mind, intelligence, and false ego] of the living entities. There is no other way than this."

The holy name will lighten your load, shorten your time to perfection, and comfort you in need. As you listen to the interior conversation the chanting of the Name facilitates, you'll begin to recognize the authentic, reliable inner voice, trust it, and increase its volume. Further, the Name makes you more disposed to *act* on the guidance. We need all this assistance to completely efface the false ego. This is the most important and difficult undertaking any of us will ever tackle. And it's an absolute requirement for genuine progress.

In addition to the work of ego effacement, Sri Nama will also show you all the good in you and how you can carry your qualities forward to a more active role in your daily life. And, of course, the Names will guide you in more than just psychological health; they will show you how to structure both your attitude and your practice in ways that are most suitable for your ultimate spiritual success.

As the ego dissolves, remembrance of your Divine Friend – initiated and fueled by chanting his holy names and hearing about him – increases and becomes constant. Constant remembrance is the goal of a kirtan practice. In *The Sonic Thread,* Cynthia Snodgrass writes, "To remember continually is to be touched continually by divine forces that enliven the heart and remembering this brings bliss and the blessings of divine communion."

Remembering lets us "see again," but to see what we now wish to remember doesn't require that we first used our eyes. We can re-see something we heard. The ears are the "eyes" we use to perceive the Divine, and one who chants the maha-mantra in earnest experiences the power of the ears to see because so many realizations about the Divine and vistas of transcendence are shown to the chanter.

As valuable as all these realizations are, we want to have a direct experience of our Divine Friend. We do want to *see* him. We want to reach the fulfillment of our spiritual aspirations. However, we will not see with the material eyes, which are incapable of perceiving spirit. Proper hearing opens our spiritual eyes by purifying the heart and dispensing with the false sense of self. When the eyes of the soul open, we'll see our Divine Friend directly. It's when our heart melts and, in great separation, we develop an intense desire to see our Friend that he will appear before us and assuage our angst.

In his *Dig-Darshini-Tika,* Sanatana Goswami – the bhakti mystic we met in chapter five, who gave away the touchstone – says kirtan of the Names is the supreme method for directly seeing Krishna. Actually, he says, it is the *only* method. If we want to see the Supreme Person someday, we'll do kirtan. And our kirtan is helped when we fix the beautiful form of Sri Krishna in the mind and then *pray* the mantra with deep longing. We'll first see the form of Sri Krishna in the mind by hearing about his form, qualities, and activities from sacred texts, then through a kirtan practice we will see him directly. As thoughts become fully absorbed in the Supreme a spontaneous free flow of love will begin.

At a certain point in your yoga practice the work of stripping back the masks and layers of the false self is complete and the mind stops harassing you and squandering your precious energy. The insecurities, fears, illusions, desires, grief, frustrations, and anger lift away and you become self-composed and disimpassioned in all circumstances. You come to rest in the self, who is by nature pure, joyful, illumined, and immortal. Like a mystic, you experience the unity – the brotherhood and sisterhood – of all life and act compassionately in the world. Your conduct, character, and consciousness have changed permanently.

This state of being is not beyond you. It is a natural benefit of a prema-kirtan practice. Of course, the ego isn't dismantled in a day or a month or even a year. Sustained effort is needed. We all know that to achieve anything in life takes effort, determination, focus, and patience. Therefore we chant the maha-mantra daily and are committed to a long-term practice.

To keep the mantra breathing within us we need to lend it our breath and chant always. Repeat it over and over; use all the moments between the busyness of your life to say the mantra. Lead your kirtan into single-hearted meditation, with full absorption in the Supreme, and he will, in time, show himself to you.

The Heartfulness Beyond Mindfulness

We've been talking about controlling the mind, a task required for any spiritual practice to be successful. But bhakti yoga is not simply about stilling or quieting the mind; it's about engaging the mind in ways that evoke the soul's innate loving nature. That requires that we fill the mind with spiritual content that inspires the heart and spiritualizes the mind and senses. Bhakti is, in that sense, a path of the heart. The focus isn't solely on mindfulness but heartfulness.

At the substratum of existence lives the collective heart – the primordial heart of the Eternal Person from whom the self receives its emotional capacity and qualities. It is this Person who makes our true heart beat – something we'll recognize when we align and harmonize with him. Heartfulness is a faculty of the self seeking connection with its whole state; it's the self expressing itself in relationship to the Whole, of whom each of us is an individual, atomic part, like rays of a grand sun.

Mindfulness in itself cannot satisfy the self. We as a society have long focused on the mind-body instead of the heart as the channel to spirit, proven by the extensive protocols our society has developed for achieving mental health and overall physical and emotional well-being. If this were enough, why are we still unsatisfied? Doc Childre writes in *The HeartMath Solution,* "Even longtime meditators get only limited benefits unless the heart is deeply engaged, so they're often frustrated with their progress."

Mindfulness is awareness tethered to the temporal "now." Although living in the moment is calming, the moment is still fleeting, and remaining ever in the "now" is not a sustainable state of being. One "now" is replaced by another and another – a new "now" at every moment. Because there is no permanent "now," this type of meditation is an attempt (largely unsuccessful) at mental control that is mixed with a fair dose of self-encouragement. In the end, mindfulness can only engage the self partially. In fact, as we've discussed, the mind is a covering over the self we need to free ourselves of. We don't want to only still and control the mind, we want to supplant it!

The self is the *possessor* of the mind; therefore the self is more important than the mind, which needs to be used in our best interest. For these and other reasons, mindfulness can bring mental calm, but little more.

The self is all heart. At the center of our being is love. Therefore heartfulness, not mindfulness, makes us whole and answers the human beings' perennial questions about why I exist and what is the meaning of my life. The self controls the mind; the self expresses heart.

But lest we misunderstand, bhakti is not a mindless approach. We use the mind and intellect, reason and logic, to understand the bhakti philosophy rooted in the Bhakti Vedanta texts like the Bhagavad Gita and Srimad-Bhagavatam. The essence of bhakti is to live a wise existence in which we know our relationship with our Divine Other and joyfully participate in that loving relationship. We engage the whole self: mind and heart. Bhakti is not sentimentality and emotionalism but a *harmonizing* of head and heart. On firm philosophical ground we use our head (intellect) to change us (heart). We want genuine spiritual emotion grounded in knowledge of self-truth and Reality; we want to love wisely and act wisely so that we may become happy.

Heartfulness, bhakti, is a function of the mind and heart becoming one in focus on loving the perfect object of love. It's mindfulness with emotions registered with absolute feeling for the Supreme Person, whose grand cosmic heart is the source of the purest love.

Just as we need mental focus to practice mindfulness, so we need to focus the heart's attention to practice heartfulness. *Single-heartedness* means to clear the heart of all the false loves and false values that currently fill it and moor it instead to the Supreme Person. Part of our self-reflection will include removing the false loves from our heart. Then we can have single-mindedness because the mind follows the heart. This is how we control the mind and propel our progress. And when we sync the heart with its origin – the source of the cosmic heartbeat – then pure feeling flows, envelops us, and spreads out to heal everyone we contact.

Heartfulness in bhakti is a way of being in the world that carries us beyond the celestial ceiling into the realm of selfless divine love, the world of Reality and the eternal present. The mental plane, whether we've tamed it or not, has no access to that world. Only the heart can lead us beyond the land of matter into the land of love. You could say that heartfulness is the process by which we activate the eternal heart.

In addition to how our hearts are shut down to spiritual truths and activities and thus dead to our true self and our root Source, even in ordinary affairs we often ignore the sensing we receive through the material heart, but if we activate that sensing capacity it can help us identify and hone the spiritual perception.

Modern society has numbed our ability to be heartful to the point that we hardly remember we have this precious, innate sensing capacity. The heart is an organ of perception, and we've nearly forgotten its value and how to use it. It's very capable of feeling and hearing messages from the intelligence of all the life that surrounds us. This sensing gives life meaning. When we open ourselves to sensing with the heart, we will learn to hear its messages.

Heart sensing means to "touch" the world with the capacities of the heart. By paying attention to the messages of the world – by tuning into the world around us with the sensing faculty of the heart, we're able to perceive what the other senses miss. What we recognize through heart sensing comes from carefully paying attention and "listening" to the environment, ourselves, and other beings.

For instance, recently, a woman I'd never met came to my home to pick up something I'd sold her online. We timed our meeting based on her husband's schedule, as he was a busy lawyer. She was punctual, well-dressed, and cordial. Visually, she didn't appear like someone who would be sensitive to these ideas of heartfulness, so what happened was unexpected. As she walked around with me to the side of my house, she slowed, then stopped, and placed her hand on her heart almost as if her breath was taken away. I stopped with her, a little concerned. Quite embarrassed she said, "I'm sorry. I'm feeling something and it's a little overwhelming. I need to compose myself.... It seems you're doing something very special here."

Of course, my home is an ashram where we've done kirtan and japa for decades. To me it seemed she had been paying attention to her heart sense and was able to pick up on the spiritual energy of my home. The spiritual energy of the place had literally stopped her in her tracks because she was paying attention.

This heart sensing occurs the moment you break free of the dullness, the superficial, the purely external, to *feel*. You do more than see the room you've just entered, hear the crackle in the fireplace, see the winter sunlight peeking in, and smell the tea on the stove.

You become aware of the feeling communication coming to you when you come upon an ancient live oak that has recently toppled and is sprawled on the ground or you enter a vast field of freshly bloomed, vibrant black-eyed Susans. You feel fully when you sense the mood of that house with the large sun painted on the front door, or the mature, high, flexible bamboo swaying in the summer breeze.

Heart sensing is paying attention to how you're touched as you perceive the world; how the world is alive and speaking to you. Sri Chaitanya heard the world speaking to him and said, "Look. The grass is humble. The trees are tolerant. If you chant in this mood, you'll make rapid progress toward love of God."

This kind of knowing is desirable and supports the heartfulness of bhakti. It's different from intellectual knowing, which is where we spend most of our time and which keeps us separate from nature and ourselves and predisposes us to harm others and the environment because the mind can be heartless and selfish. But imagine if we chose instead to have an intimate exchange with everything around us through heart sensing? How *inspired* would such sensing make us? How would our ordinary and spiritual lives improve?

And what is kirtan but a heart transaction? Kirtan activates the soul's heart and arouses bhakti's heartfulness in our whole being. Beyond the movement of the music the love evoked by prema-kirtan moves us into another realm, where the heartbeat is more expansive and expressive and the feelings come from a pure heart. There the heart finds its ultimate ecstasy. Kirtan can take us there.

Kirtan artist Havi Dasa explains, "In the art of kirtan the

Absolute dimension becomes an experienced reality. This is due to the benevolent presence of God in his names. While chanting we may not be aware of all these profound truths, but the fact remains ... and ultimately kirtan is the sublime weapon that will not only destroy our misunderstandings about our identity, purify our heart, and develop our dormant love for God, but if we strive in that direction we could end up living in that transcendental realm where every word is a song and every step a dance."

It's love that calls us most strongly, and it's love that inclines the Infinite to us. St. Teresa of Avila said, "Love draws out love." The bhakti process pulls on all our love and then refines our capacity to love – augments it – and coaxes it into pure divine love. Prema is no cheap attainment, but still the method to attain it is accessible. My spiritual master assured us, "Even a child can chant."

Magical Thinking

I often meet people who are confident that when they die they'll attain a spiritual destination, whether that's heaven or some other state of happiness. We're taught that if we live clean lives and do good for others, we've done the best human beings can do, so we'll be rewarded with a spiritual attainment.

Many people think that good acts include performing daily or weekly ritual prayer or mantras, visits to churches, synagogues, or temples, or other expressions of belief in God. This moral way of being is part of spiritual progress. Yet many people still wrestle with impatience, a lack of compassion and forgiveness, envy, anger, their desire-appetites, controlling the mind, seeing other beings as equal to themselves, and other unbecoming qualities they may have. But if we're unwilling to admit these shortcomings through self-reflection and *work* in earnest to change them then we shouldn't think that the spiritual work is being completed.

Morality and virtue are beneficial to ourselves and others, but mundane piety will not open the door to the spiritual world. We gain entrance only when we have an absolute change of heart – which manifests in our behavior. What to speak of being filled with good qualities, free from vices, and transcending human passions, we will swoon in ecstatic love for the Supreme Person. Until then, we should know there is more work to do to attain a spiritual destination.

Many people acknowledge that a transcendental destination requires wholesale transformation, but they think death is the magical moment when their shortcomings are somehow erased – even if they've been unsuccessful in doing the work of making that happen during their lives. They're convinced they'll be completely altered for the better simply by dying.

All of this is to say that even the sincerest of us need a daily, genuine practice that is capable of effacing the ego; of dismantling what is unbecoming in us. It isn't true that simply by one's dying, the work is done.

Death *is* a defining point, but it's not a point where we can magically be transformed without having done our work throughout life. In the eighth chapter of the Gita Krishna explains that our thoughts at death determine our future birth. It's a tendency of the mind to follow habitual patterns, so at death we'll tend to remember our primary interest and focus in life.

We have to change the mind in life if we want to be drastically changed at death. As we've heard, chanting the maha-mantra is the easiest way to do this. Then we can be careful not to "undo" the work of the mantra by mindfully choosing what else we hear. Because the mind is disturbed by the dying process, it's difficult, if not impossible, to focus it on anything but what it's accustomed to. This is why we ought to take great care in what we hear during life – because that's what the mind will remember at that most difficult time. After all, what we hear about, look at, and therefore think about and act on is symptomatic of what we choose to invest our heart in. It is this culturing of consciousness that we foster in each lifetime that dictates our next destination.

We can take note that determination to live this advice is fortified when we remember our death is near. Sages and mystics the world over tell us to live as if the next moment is our last. Most of us prefer not to take things *that* seriously. Why should we trouble ourselves, always thinking we could die? How can we be happy thinking like that?

But did you know that in Bhutan, sometimes called the happiest place on earth, people are encouraged to think of death five times a day? Linda Leaming, author of *A Field Guide to Happiness: What I Learned in Bhutan About Living, Loving, and Waking Up*, writes, "I realised thinking about death doesn't depress me. It makes me seize the moment and see things I might not ordinarily see."

The problem is, we consider such thinking unnecessary. We haven't actually understood – realized – our spiritual nature and the horror of repeated birth and death. Therefore we're willing to put off or make light of what is of actual value and benefit for us.

If we take the sages' reminder seriously, we'd find it fosters in us a deep commitment to a spiritual practice and willingness to do the work of ego effacement. Such determination doesn't take away from the ability to have a happy, healthy life. It does, however, enable us take full advantage of all that a human life can grant us. For those who grasp the urgency, the mystics' reminder is helpful, because when the moment of death arrives, we want to be as prepared as possible to consciously step over the head of death. This is an extraordinary goal that is so rarely achieved because few are willing to make the commitment.

"If it's rare," you might counter, "why bother trying for it?" Krishna replies in the Gita that there is no loss in an earnest attempt in bhakti. This is not the case with partial progress made in the other yogas, which are all material processes for controlling the mind. If the practitioner doesn't achieve perfection in this life, they begin anew in the next. Progress we make in bhakti, however, is never diminished because bhakti is a spiritual energy and therefore is imperishable. It is permanent. And even the slightest practice saves us from the greatest danger, which is rebirth in an animal species. However far we progress in this life, we'll continue from that point in the next. But with no effort made we could lose our chance at higher consciousness now and in the future. So we try our best and pray for grace. Mercy comes. Magic happens.

Chapter 7

A KIRTAN CULTURE

Desiring to bless all living entities,
this sweet name of Krishna
has descended to this material universe and shines,
like the sun in the sky of the heart,
destroying the darkness of ignorance.
– Thakura Bhaktivinoda

As important as it is that we fill the mind with spiritual content, it's just as important to control the input of mundane sound. For instance, I don't own a television. What a relief it is to be free of the newscasters' intentional attempts to create fear and anxiety in their listeners! I don't "relax" by following social media posts, watching movies, sitcoms, series, reality shows, or YouTube videos. Actually, we can't really relax when the mind is agitated with fast-paced visual and auditory messages. Entertainment overstimulates the senses as programs or social media posts move rapidly from scene to scene or we're assaulted – and insulted – by aggressive advertising.

Television, social media, and computer games don't give us inner or outer harmony, nor can they give our lives meaning and balance. The images flood the mind, choke it, and cause it to sink into whirlpools of fear, anxiety, and mundane impressions that call us to consume and try to enjoy more or in ways we hadn't thought of, further enshrining the false self or false ego and false values. Instead of developing a strong yearning to transcend our conditioning and become liberated from the dictates of the mind, this type of input suffocates our spiritual instinct and saps enthusiasm to practice yoga.

We just heard how what we hear determines our thoughts at death, and in chapter three we discussed how what we hear, what we ingest into the mind, fashions the mind along with our intuition and intelligence just as food shapes the nature and health of the physical body. Giving the mind real food will energize us and make us healthy and happy; feeding the mind junk food will deaden the mental and intellectual faculties and leave us feeling a bit ill. Further, by ingesting media junk, we're undoing the spiritual work we may have done or, at least, making the work much more difficult. We're already living in a virtual reality because we're under the illusion that we're the mind-body. We don't need to add layers to that virtual landscape and become further distant from ourselves by regularly entering the world of media.

We let ourselves be taken in by media because we seek to escape from something in our lives or in ourselves. We *hope* to be distracted. I understand. I owned a TV in the past; there were times when I *needed* to escape from my life. But if we examine what's transpiring in us when we watch, we'll find that it's not as much entertainment as it is *entrainment* to others' ways of thinking and behaving: we absorb what others think and do. Media often promotes competition, consumerism, and exploitation as values, and portrays fame, wealth, drinking, and casual sex as sources of happiness, but all these have been proven to be bankrupt – ask anyone who's had them or indulged in them. You'll find they're still chasing happiness no matter how much they've had their fill.

When we spend time with devices, we're not embodying our own lives. I'll say that again: we don't fully embody our own lives.

We're generally aware that time spent like this means we're unproductive in areas of our lives that deserve our attention. Perhaps we don't exercise as we ought to, we let projects around the house slide, or we don't give our children (enough) quality time. The losses in these, and other, important areas of our lives can accumulate to be significant.

And, ultimately, we alienate ourselves from our own values and sources of happiness. In some cases we become like the people we watch and listen to – we imbibe the way they think and speak and act, although a lot of what we see is unbecoming or mean. In the most drastic examples, our children are acting out in real life the violence they see on TV and computer games. Their violence with guns has forever changed that we thought our children were safe in schools. And now we're finding more and more people who are addicted to devices wrestling with compulsions for unwholesome content like graphic sex where women's bodies are objectified, and the sexual act demeaned.

Better we embody our own life, not give it away to someone or something else. To embody life means to live it with depth, contemplating the nature of the self and of Reality. You're not going to find yourself by watching or listening to media. And anyway, the escape is never complete or even fully satisfying. Rather, it simply kills time when we don't really know what else to do with ourselves.

But by killing time we rob ourselves of opportunities to find freedom from the control of time. Time and space are unwelcome, unnecessary limitations on the soul. If we want to become unfettered from these shackles, we have to consciously participate in practical activities that have the power to release the self. We need quality time with the self to get to know the self. We also need time to be able to realize the self. Escaping into mundane media may let us feel – for a few moments – that we're liberated from the demands of the time and space of our immediate lives, but this is a grand illusion. Time is a supreme controller; it is colossal: from a blink to the passing of millennia and millennia.

The Bhagavata (2.3.17) says, "Both by rising and by setting, the sun decreases the duration of life of everyone, except one who utilizes the time by discussing topics of the all-good Personality of Godhead." A. C. Bhaktivedanta Swami comments, "Even a fraction of the duration of life wasted cannot be compensated by any amount of gold. Human life is simply awarded to a living entity (atma) so that he can realize his spiritual identity and his permanent source of happiness."

The body-mind is a sophisticated instrument capable of revealing profound insights into the human condition and the nature of the soul if we use the faculties in a spiritual practice designed to reveal the self. We need stretches of time to sit and be with ourselves without input from others, without being assaulted with insidious ideas about buying, consuming, and doing. When we tune out the opinions, expectations, and obligations of the world around us, we begin to hear ourselves and can contemplate the deeper questions about life and our own existence.

Instead of looking to media to lighten the intensity of a stressful life, perhaps we can rethink how we're living. Maybe we don't need as many things – perhaps we don't need a house as large as we think or a fancy car which cost more than we can actually afford; or maybe we don't need to push for the higher position at work. We may not really have to accomplish so much, although we're trained from birth to think we're failures if we don't have enough ambition. We should have ambition, but ambition for what? It's more common than you might think to have mistaken ideas about what brings happiness. Yet all of us concur that it's not the externals that enrich us as much as a peaceful mind, healthy body, and loving relationships. Still, we chase other things – things that won't really make us happy. This is called ignorance.

Let's escape instead into the enthralling, meaningful life of the Absolute. Instead of talking about, hearing about, watching movies about, hearing songs about, and reading day in and day out about the possessions, (ill) behaviors, destinations, food, drink, things, and sex lives of so many (mostly fictional) characters, we can talk about, hear about, and read about the Eternal Person, the Lord of Love, who is full of a variety of activities, is the very form of bliss, beauty, and knowledge, and who has invited us to join him in loving exchanges.

A mantra meditation practice can free us from the oppressive demands of mundane media as it makes its demands on our intellect and heart, on our very self. The freer we make our mind, the more capacity we'll have for meditation.

At the least, by beginning to cultivate a mantra meditation

practice we'll be able to wean ourselves off some portion of our life-sapping interaction with mundane media. We can wrest back control of our precious self and decide on the content of our thoughts and emotions. However much time we can steal back from the media, we can use to gradually increase our yoga practice – simply by choosing what we hear.

Dying in a Kirtan Culture

Among my friends who've taken up mantra meditation as a practice there's an abiding commitment to be present for each other when we die. Death is the most important moment of life in the sense that all our practices, prayers, and spiritual hopes lead to this crucial aspiration: let me remember Krishna as I die. If I can remember him as I take my last breath, if I can have his names on my lips as I breathe my last, he has promised to personally come for me. Krishna gives himself to those who express this love: I will use all my breaths, including my last, to call your name.

Why would someone be *so* devoted? Because they love him! Kirtan has aroused such a deep love for him in them – a love that had long been buried beneath an avalanche of false loves, false dreams, false values, and selfish desires.

What kind of relationship can you have with someone you've devoted everything to? A passionate and intimate one.

In your final bed, as you prepare to leave aside your body, you'll know how much of your heart you've held back by what you find yourself absorbed in. We want death to be a moment of triumph; we know the moment is trying and we need help. For me and my friends, it's an honor to serve one another in our striving for the rare attainment of pure love. So how to die is actually part of culturing kirtan, and it's common in the bhakti culture to hold festivals of the holy name at one another's deathbed.

The more our realization of the self and our relationship with the Supreme increases, we'll find that chanting is making us fearless. The theoretical knowledge that we're not the body-mind complex becomes lived – known fully – and we lose our fear of death and other types of loss. Everything happening to us here, in this world, is external to the self, that unit of spirit, untouched by time and matter, this is the deeper truth. Before we reach this direct knowing, we can remind ourselves of this truth throughout all our life experiences.

Like many people my age, I've lost many lifelong friends. We've stayed by each person, chanting kirtan and reading bhakti texts to them. At the moment someone departs, we let our kirtan soar in simultaneous sadness and joy, and the sound of our heartfelt union increases as we send them forward with affection.

Many of us raised our families together, took vacations together, celebrated the birth of our children, holidays, anniversaries, holy days, and festivals together. We dedicated ourselves to careers and worked for the good of the wider community. Throughout it all we also remained committed to our kirtan and japa practices, oftentimes meeting together to practice, because *sanga,* or the support of others who walk our path, is crucial in the practice of bhakti. We helped one another not neglect the inner pilgrimage and the imperative to prepare for the next life.

In essence it could be said that we lived two lives – the one everyone lives, and the one few choose to live – and achieved the advantages of both. Both material and spiritual pursuits are work, but if you choose to work only for a material life, you lose everything: at death you don't take anything with you but your accumulated karma. If you choose only a material life and neglect your inner development, you'll die only to be reborn again. To a spiritualist this is living as if you've never lived because you missed the aim of human life: to become free from the material entanglement. If you live spiritual practices, even if you don't perfect them in this life, you pick up where you left off – your realization and progress isn't lost with the death of the body – so there's no loss. Better we choose to live the life of the heart by simply incorporating kirtan and japa into our lives.

It's gratifying beyond words to devote yourself to the inner journey, have fellow sojourners with whom you can compare notes about the obstacles, beauty, and surprises along the way and with whom you regularly share kirtan and japa, relish intriguing philosophical discussions, and engage your talents in ways that express your devotional heart. Such a life has so much meaning. How, then, can I describe what occurs when we sit with a friend as we help them try to launch themselves into the plane of existence beyond the mundane? How can I put into words the depth of gratitude one feels as one stands witness to a life worthy of being lived and cheers that soul onward? It's a beautiful way to leave the body. If you like, you can make a similar commitment to your friends and family and ask that kirtan be part of your own rite of passage.

I want to take special note here that the holy names of the maha-mantra are different from other mantras. If we've cultivated a relationship with the Names in sadhana and genuinely done the inner work chanting brought up for us, then the person in the mantra will present himself to our awareness at that crucial moment even if we are ourselves unable to pronounce the mantra.

It's by grace that we receive a spiritual body and identity. I've been speaking of the work we must do because our effort is a practical demonstration of our sincerity and desire – a demonstration of devotion and love. Ultimately, however, we're dependent on grace. Grace, we learn from bhakti texts, is Krishna reciprocating our love. Thus we have our own participation in grace.

From our side we call out with feeling as we chant the holy names, throwing up both arms in surrender as Queen Draupadi did. Draupadi appears in the epic *Mahabharata,* the romantic, sociopolitical drama that nestles the Gita in its pages. She had five powerful husbands. Any one of them could have physically protected her, but a circumstance arose in which all of them were helpless. She was pulled into the throne room, where her husbands sat, humiliated, and a huge warrior pulled on her sari to disrobe her in front of her husbands' enemies. At first Draupadi tried to grab hold of her sari to stop from being stripped, but realizing she was powerless, she raised one hand in the air and called out, "O Krishna, please help me!" Again she realized how futile it was to pit her strength against this mammoth attacking her, so she released her sari altogether and threw up both arms, again crying for help. Krishna responded by mystically supplying an unlimited length of sari cloth, making it impossible for the warrior to disrobe her.

We want to create an altar in the heart and invite our Divine Friend to sit there. Our Friend wants to know how much we want his participation in our lives, and how much we trust him. We're habituated to ignoring him and have done so for a very long time. When we do pay him a little attention, once we get what we want from him we go on about our lives and, by our behavior, ask him to also be on his way as we return to ignoring him. We should be careful of this mood when practicing meditation on the holy name. Certainly we don't want to develop a relationship with the person of the mantra, then send him away whenever his presence seems unnecessary or inconvenient – we want to keep both hands raised in supplication and submission fully depending on grace. Of course, many of us have the tendency to dispense with God when we've had our fill, even if we don't always recognize it in ourselves. We see this everywhere, and it's graphically on display in India.

Every year, millions of people worship Durga, Shiva, or Ganesh by calling them into a deity sculpted particularly for a festival, at which they ask for boons. A few days later, when their festival is complete, priests recite mantras, asking the deity, "Now please go back." They then take the deity and throw it in a lake or the ocean to dispose of it. This is so prevalent in India that the disposal of the *murtis* pollutes rivers and lakes and regularly generates an outcry from concerned citizens and government officials. This self-serving "bhakti" is unbecoming and offers meager, material benefits and increasing material problems beyond only polluting lakes and rivers.

When we lean into our Friend as our only shelter, as Draupadi did, we show him that we trust him and that he can trust us – we're not going to periodically throw him away. Love, after all, is reciprocal. We want his love, and he wants ours. When we become trustworthy, he gives himself to us in love and invites us home.

If you're inclined to ask entry into the living world, then singing and dancing in prema-kirtan, following the ways of spiritually alive people, is your way. However, because Sri Krishna is subjugated by love and gives himself over completely in love, this crest jewel of all spiritual attainments is not easily achieved. The price we must pay is intense eagerness and longing to reach him. This is best cultured in good company.

Sanga, the Company We Keep

An important part of the successful culture of bhakti is keeping company with serious practitioners who share our ideal – we need friends, mentors, and guides. The world is elegantly designed to keep us bound to it without us recognizing all the subtle ways we're tied by illusion. We may know theoretically that we're not the mind-body, but we don't act as if we *know* that. Theoretical knowledge and realized knowledge are very different, and there's no short cut to experiential spirituality. To gain first-hand experience – and thereby realized knowledge – takes time and practice.

I have succumbed to the call of the world many times without realizing it. Other times, I couldn't recognize that certain thoughts and behaviors were tainted by self-interest or some other motive contrary to the goal of my bhakti practice. I encountered stages in my sadhana that I thought were something to be concerned about but, when understood in reference to sacred texts and the experience of mystics, were actually indications of progress.

I've seen a number of practitioners get hung up on details and lose sight of the essence, perhaps focusing on rules instead of principles or becoming consumed by dogma and fanaticism instead of living spirituality; I and so many others I've known over the years have sometimes missed the distinction between relative and absolute considerations. I can't count the number of times that my understanding has been edified and enlarged – despite my attempt over the years to immerse myself in deep study and practice – by mentors, gurus, and fellow practitioners. They have helped me unravel all sorts of things and understand layers of meaning.

In short, the journey we undertake in the yoga of kirtan on the path of bhakti is tailored to each individual. Your journey is a universe unto itself. We're navigating a landscape we've never traversed before. We shouldn't expect to traverse such a path without companions and guides. To see Oz behind the curtain requires help from friends, as Toto showed Dorothy in *The Wizard of Oz*.

As smart as we are, we really don't know everything. In fact, we know little about spirit or even the behind-the-scenes workings of material nature. Those who experience the power of the mantra and want to become more serious about their practice will search out a competent guru.

Imagine facing an untamed jungle that is miles and miles wide. How do you cut your way through? How much labor is involved? How much danger are you in as, without power tools or machines, you break through growths of small trees, thick brush, shrubs, vines, overhanging tree branches, climb over stumps and boulders, and face the elements and wild animals whose home you are invading? In such a jungle each *inch* is a dangerous distance and neither sheer brute strength nor astute intelligence assure you of success.

Now, if someone were to point out that there's already a trail, cleared long ago, and that trail has been kept open so that anyone can walk on it, then wouldn't you choose that trail instead of trying to carve a new one? After all, there's no guarantee you'll be successful at building a unique path, even if you're willing to risk your life to do so.

Taking the established trail is known in Vedic texts as

"following the path of the *mahajanas,*" or great souls. This ancient trail is traversed by a consecutive succession of great souls who keep the path free of obstruction. There are those currently on the path who hold the map that was handed to them by those who walked before them. Such a map-bearer has news of the destination, stories about the successful passage of others, and understands the pitfalls and can offer advice how to avoid them. We need such a mahajana, not a show-bottle spiritualist or cheater. We should educate ourselves how to recognize such persons so that in our search we look for an essence-seeker and know how to examine their worthiness before accepting them as a guide.

The wisdom teacher should be pure-hearted. I mentioned earlier that a guru is a bearer of the name who can transfer the living mantra to us. Bhakti is transmitted into the heart by one who has bhakti. Continued association with such a person further nourishes the development of the seed of divine love planted in our heart. Such persons know the Bhakti Vedanta texts and are adept at explaining them. Most importantly they feel for the subject; their hearts are changed. They are detached from material possessions gross and subtle and have direct experience of the self. They can help us progress at each juncture of our lives and make sense for us of the various stages of bhakti. Such persons show us how to slake the soul's thirst as we uproot our desires to gratify the body and instead, exercise our true nature in loving service to the Supreme Person.

And we need like-minded friends with whom we can sit with to do kirtan, share festival days, speak with about the novel experiences we're each having, and encourage each other as we encounter challenges.

Intentional Meditation

As we heard in chapter four, our intention influences whether we'll receive the full effects of the power of sacred sound. I embrace the holy names as nondifferent from the Supreme Person in a mood of humility and service, carefully trying to understand my true identity as spirit separate from the mind-body. Humility and service are the qualities that take us to the land of the soul, and prema-kirtan draws out these natural characteristics of the soul.

Service is an expression of love; it's synonymous with love. Calling out your beloved's name is a tangible display of love. And Krishna accepts our chanting as service. So simply by giving some of our precious time to chanting the holy names, we're engaged in a loving act of service.

Humility, or developing a humble state of mind, is the natural result of self-honesty. The atma is described in yogic texts as a finite spark of spirit. We're small sparks of a great fire, atomic units of sentience, small bits of consciousness, particles of truth. Vedanta says that there's nothing smaller in all of creation than the atma, the self. It's beneficial to remember this while we chant: we're atomic units of spirit.

Just contemplate this for a moment, and let's try to experience it through a short exercise. Once you do this, you can remember this experience before you begin your meditation (or periodically during your meditation).

You don't have to be able to "see" all aspects of the following exercise; just get a general feel of dimension and distance relative to the objects discussed. Think loosely about these things and try to draw up the general vision as you read. It's best to bring into your vision a *feeling* for your size. Perhaps marvel at the scale of sizes, your size, and how you generally think of your size and importance.

Now, take a moment to think of yourself inside your home. How much space does your body occupy there? Perhaps you can close your eyes for a second and feel your size relative to your house. Now think of the size of your house relative to the town it's in. How does the town's size correspond to the size of the state, and the state's to the continent? How does this affect the feeling of your own size? Hold these spatial relationships in mind as you continue to locate yourself in the universe. Remember your size in relation to the size of the continent. Go farther out and think of your place on earth. Perhaps you can bring up a mental image of earth from space and allow yourself to *feel* your size in relation to the earth within the expanding universe. For perspective, remember that the earth is 93 million miles from the sun. The Milky Way alone contains an estimated 800 billion planets; there are as many as 6 billion earthlike planets in our galaxy – and there are estimates of between 200 billion to 2 trillion galaxies, each with its own contingent of planets. Where are you? How big are you?

What's more astounding is that Vedanta says there are unlimited universes like our universe!

Yet we think of ourselves as large. We want to be big, although we're small. This inner battle creates anxiety, fear, insecurity, and a host of psychological and spiritual problems. Acknowledging your smallness encourages simplicity and humility – an attractive innocence that frees up space in your mind and heart for what has real meaning: loving relationships with our self, others, and the Supreme. Importantly, the willingness to acknowledge your smallness and your interdependent relationship with others grants you peace and softens your heart. If you can tune into this frequency, you can become an instrument of love and bring harmony into your life and the lives of others.

This meditation shows that we're not the Whole but only a part of the Whole, and as a part we have an intrinsic relationship with the Whole.

Of course, some people feel a need to assert themselves over others because the world is a dangerous place of exploitation. But our attempt to secure ourselves by this means does not work, because we're not all-powerful, nor are we in control. Therefore we're advised to give up this approach if we want to arrive at our true position. But what about our safety? We come to realize that nothing material can protect us – not even an assertive attitude and assured competence. It is only in cultivating our relationship with the Whole, who is fully capable of protecting us, that we can find ultimate security against the unlimited dangers of this world.

Now, it's equally important to recognize something else about yourself: in fact, you *are* large – larger than any material object, planet, or galaxy. As a unit of consciousness, you have meaning and purpose in a manner no material, temporary thing has. You have immense value. The atma is the object in this world that's loveable. In that sense you're the biggest. As a unit of spirit, you're naturally a lover, and as such have inestimable value to the Supreme Person and all other atmas. When you understand your true nature, and focus on purifying and melting your heart, you can shine in your own true worth.

Knowing our spiritual nature and embracing a humble state of mind can free us from our constant pursuit of things and status. Humility inspires us to want to take less, consume less, demand less. A humble state of mind facilitates the step-by-step process of dissolving the false ego by inclining us to remove from ourselves our separatist interests and all else that's selfish. We'll think of ourselves less and of others more. We'll live more intentionally and become more thoughtful, agreeable, and compassionate. And by drawing up humility for chanting we find we can be used as an instrument of meaningful service in the world.

The internal shift that occurs when we embrace our small-ness fills us with deep peace. As we choose to recognize that we're neither self-created nor self-contained nor self-sustained, and we chant with the humility that stems from knowing we're dependent on the Supreme Person, who loves us, we find our-selves secure in a way that no material status, wealth, knowl-edge, relationship, or possession – all of which are temporary and can be taken from us at any time – can give us. This mood evokes love in us because our honesty and vulnerability – the courage to be small and imperfect – attracts our Beloved to us. When we need him, he will come.

Brené Brown became famous by observing and articulating the ways that vulnerability gives us intimacy and depth in rela-tionships. Of course, being vulnerable is a frightening prospect in relationship with other human beings who can misunder-stand and abuse us, but this potential drawback does not exist in relation with the Supreme Person. We can come before the Beloved vulnerable, as we actually are, and be loved, safely and wholly.

Accepting our atomic finiteness tremendously benefits our mantra meditation. We begin to sense what it means to call out in earnest, because we feel completely dependent. If some-one is fully dependent on you and sincerely petitions you, with appreciation for all that you do and genuinely praises your good qualities, isn't it natural that you'll open your heart to them? Krishna responds in compelling ways. He makes himself unfailingly, unconditionally available to you. The Gita says that Krishna reciprocates with us according to how we approach him. This honors our agency as individual selves – he lets us choose the degree of exchange we want with him. So your relationship with your Source depends on how you approach him.

Through prema-kirtan and japa we develop our inner ear, our inner receptivity, our ability to hear him and to see the Reality beyond the veil of illusion. Through meditation on the holy names you get to know the Supreme Person – you start a dialogue that will form the most important conversation of your life.

There's no need to rush the process. The communication will give you the wings to soar, and as its quality increases, you will soar beyond all misidentification with matter into the world of truth. Everything is possible through chanting Hare Krishna. Be attentive and hear the names; take Sri Nama with you everywhere.

Sri Nama will reveal more and more to you, until one day you wake from the dream.

Chapter 8

SOUNDS OF TRANSFORMATION

*All of reality is but different notes harmonizing together
in one song: the song of life beyond the graveyard
of material existence. Those who ignore this – the tone deaf –
will never dance in the land of eternal life.*
– Swami Tripurari

Each of us is a particle of spirit and belongs to the higher world
of consciousness, where love never falters. It's time to go home.

You can, however, choose otherwise. Will you stay in the
earthly realm, where you're born and die repeatedly? Will you
strive to become disembodied and merge into the impersonal
oneness, to slide into a deep sleep for eternity? Will you be
granted an immortal spiritual body qualified to exchange in an
infinite ocean of loving pastimes with your Divine Friend – a
feeling, conscious person?

Beyond time, in the land of Goloka (Krishna's home in
the spiritual plane), we roam carefree and answer the need of
the heart by exchanging in blissful relationships with trusted
people of exceptional qualities, each of whom has made Sri

Krishna the center of their life, thereby participating in a harmonious environment of unity in love.

Intimacy between the Supreme and the souls reaches its zenith when the Supreme personally appears – attracted by the unalloyed love of his devotees – and plays among them as if he were human. Concealing his supremacy in the land of prema, Sri Krishna lives and behaves with his devotees as if there were no difference between them.

One established in the brilliance, purity, and power of the true self, one who has developed love for the Supreme Person is welcomed there. The soul is full of elevated qualities and excellent behavior. Such persons speak sweetly, are patient, charitable, compassionate, simple, steady, truthful, equal to all, expert, friendly, faultless, sober, kind, magnanimous, merciful, mild, peaceful, humble, poetic, do not quarrel or hanker for material things, are respectful, sane, self-controlled and – especially – are completely surrendered in love to the Supreme Person.

This is who we are in our pure state.

As we've heard, a committed practice of prema-kirtan has the power to deconstruct our material sense of self and allow us to claim our pure spiritual identity. Step by step we'll align with the true self. Kirtan is the music that takes us as its instrument – our voices and hearts – to play the music of divine love for all to hear.

This isn't poetic fancy. Through the power and grace of Sri Nama we become mystics and transcend our mere humanness and the passions that control us. This is possible. We have the capacity. And it's work – a worthy, glorious undertaking – work that is joyously filled with song and dance, work that becomes easy when we finally get the hang of letting go of resistance.

Developing a spiritual body and identity is not a minor adjustment to our thinking and being in this world; nor can we achieve it simply by willing it. We'll have to change in a most fundamental way. As we continue with our daily mantra meditation practice, we'll test the quality of our devotion by turning inward to examine our motives and the things we say and do and feel. In our daily quest to stand in the self, we'll determinedly correct thoughts, choose words, and adjust our actions. When we fail, we simply try again – and petition for help.

The Person We Become

When I speak of a new identity, I don't mean a new, better version of yourself as you know yourself in this body. I'm referring to your true self, the self that will ultimately inhabit a transcendental body, with spiritual senses, have unique characteristics, traits, and personality and live in the eternal, spiritual world. I'm speaking of a very different, extraordinary reality, a transphenomenal, transpsychological existence and a transcendental, eternal, extraordinary version of you.

To develop this identity through mantra meditation is gradual but tangible. I truly am a vastly different person from who I was five years ago, and that person was different from the person I was five years earlier, and so on. You will experience the internal change that manifests in your external behaviors and welcome the person you're becoming. You'll transform and feel deeply rewarded by that. It's one of the most gratifying experiences in life to rise beyond one's lower nature and gain mastery over oneself. This happens both for our highest good and is the best thing we can offer those we love and the planet.

In addition to the power of the maha-mantra and our work of effacing the false self, there's another component to identity creation. Let's consider how our current identity has been constructed.

We use our senses and mind to contact external sense objects so we can gratify the gross physical senses (the eyes, ears, nose, tongue, genitals, and skin) and thereby gain knowledge and gratify the mind. "Sense objects" encompasses everything in the environment. Unfortunately, for most of us, "objects" also include other people and other living beings. We use people and things to satisfy ourselves both physically and psychologically. In other words, we employ the facilities of the mind-body vehicle to draw objects to us and fill some need we're feeling. Therefore in both action and intention we center our world on the mind-body – around the small "my." Our cognition is tethered to the mind-body; hence the locus of our sense of "I" is the mind-body. This is how we've nourished our current identity, even though it has nothing to do with our essence.

To construct a spiritual identity we have to modify how we use the mind-body vehicle and be intentional about our motives. We will use our senses to engage with the world, but we need to do so for the pleasure of the Supreme rather than in pursuit of self-gratification. For instance, we've been speaking about how to use our ears in bhakti by choosing what we hear and by hearing kirtan and japa, classes about bhakti, and songs about bhakti, and by reading sacred texts. We can engage the tongue in speaking about spiritual topics, chanting, and eating food that has been first offered to the Supreme. When I have a meal, I remember that I'm taking sanctified food that will spiritualize my senses and is fuel for the body, allowing me to engage in acts of service to my Divine Friend and in a spiritual practice tailored to uplift me. There are many ways to use the body with the aim of serving the Supreme. And when our acts inevitably produce fruits – benefits such as wealth, assets, fame, etc. – we don't claim them as our own; they were produced for our Beloved.

By placing the Source at the center of our lives through this adjustment of mind and heart, a new identity manifests that's in relation to our Beloved. In this way, we spiritualize the mind and senses and cultivate affection for the Supreme that gradually matures into love. Love calls Krishna to us. It is by his grace that he grants the spiritual body and identity we're attempting to develop. The Bhagavata (5.5.6) underscores this point: "As long as one does not develop love for me, Vasudeva [Krishna], one cannot be freed from the connection with a material body."

Putting our Supreme Source at the center of our lives also completely fulfills our desire for gratification and happiness, which is what drives us so relentlessly at the moment to focus on the mind-body vehicle.

We know the feeling of joy and deep satisfaction when we do things to please those whom we love, so the concept isn't foreign to us. When the person we're trying to satisfy is the Supreme who is the very form of love, joy, beauty, harmony, and truth – who is an unlimited ocean of ecstatic emotion – we find unending joyful harmony and supreme satisfaction. When we face this prospect in earnest, we want to give more than our very self. But we only have the self to offer, so we give that fully and swim in an ocean of happiness.

Growing Affection and The Angst of Separation

I'd like to bring your attention to another mood that can power your bhakti practice. To do so, let's get further acquainted with Sri Chaitanya, whom you met briefly in the second chapter as the sixteenth-century father and inaugurator of prema-kirtan's sonic spirituality.

At the end of the Gita, Krishna implores all, "You are very well loved by me, so I shall speak for your good. Be mindful of me and devoted to me, offer to me, bow to me. You will come to me alone. I promise you this truly, for I love you. Give up all dharmas [duties], come alone to me for shelter. I shall free you from all evils, do not worry."

To remove all doubt about this instruction and the way toward our highest attainment and model how to approach the goal, Krishna re-appeared in the guise of his own devotee as Sri Chaitanya Mahaprabhu. He spread prema-kirtan, the spiritual practice for this current cosmic age and exemplified the way of a bhakti practice. Specifically, Mahaprabhu embodied the sublime mood of Sri Radha, Krishna's feminine counterwhole and the personification of prema. Because Radha is the supreme and perfect lover, her example best demonstrates how to approach the Divine. But she is hidden in the pure world beyond our purview. Therefore Sri Chaitanya came before our view embracing and exemplifying Sri Radha's state of mind to bring attention to her exalted love and show us the way to that state. In this manner, he indicates how we can progress toward Krishna.

One of Radha's states of mind is called, in the yoga literature, *vipralambha,* "separation." Mahaprabhu taught through both his words and his example that feelings of separation from the Beloved draw the Beloved close. If we're separated from someone we love, our love for them – and theirs for us – increases. Recognizing and feeling our separation from our Beloved Friend is a powerful way to nourish and grow prema. In his own ocean of love for Krishna, in Radha's mood, Sri

Chaitanya piteously petitioned everyone around him, "Where is Krishna? Where is Krishna?"*

Like Sri Radha, Chaitanya was wholly consumed by his search for Krishna. He wanted only to be united with his Beloved in loving service, and his example shows that the loving petition made in maha-mantra kirtan and japa is a potent, dynamic call to the Beloved. When we see everything related to Krishna but don't see Krishna directly, we feel separation from him. For Sri Chaitanya, everything he saw around him reminded him of Krishna, and that maddened him with ecstasy, adding intensity to his feelings of separation. The sound of a flute carried by the wind reminded him of Krishna. A forest path, a river, a flower garden, birds singing – all aroused memories of Krishna's abode and his divine activities there.

How do we see Krishna in the world? In the tenth chapter of the Gita, Krishna lists all sorts of ways he's present in the world. He speaks of all that is powerful in nature, all that is beautiful, all that is impressive in any way. When we remember these representations of Krishna, our awareness of Krishna's presence and our feelings for him can increase.

In the Gita Krishna says of the senses he is the mind; he is the consciousness in living beings; of elements he is fire; of bodies of water he is the ocean; he is the transcendental vibration om; and of sacrifices the chanting of japa. He is the taste of water.

When you drink water, you can think of him. When we think of the power of our mind we can think of it being a representation of Krishna's power. When we think of consciousness,

---

* See the found poem, "The Ecstasy of Separation," in the appendix to read of Sri Chaitanya's ecstatic feelings of separation.

life, we can remember that Krishna is the giver of life. When we look out at an ocean with seemingly endless scope we can think of unlimited Krishna.

Of immovable things he is the Himalayas; among men he is the monarch, of weapons the thunderbolt, among subduers time. Among beasts he is the lion, of purifiers the wind, of fish the shark, of rivers the mighty Ganges. He is the sound in ether, the fragrance of the earth, the heat in fire, the intelligence of the intelligent, and the ability in humankind.

Have you ever had the experience of learning something that's beyond your capacity to understand – either as a creative inspiration or insight into a puzzling problem? That is the Supreme acting in your heart. Many artists, inventors, and scientists acknowledge that their creations and insights come from beyond themselves.

In the eleventh chapter of the Gita Krishna shows Arjuna his cosmic form in matter. The sun and moon are his eyes, the hills and mountains his bones, the rivers his veins, and the trees the hairs on his body. The scorching fire of time is his mouth, the passing ages his movement, and the varieties of birds and flowers his masterful artistic sense. Since all of creation is a manifestation of his energy, we can see him everywhere.

The hills and mountains aren't literally his bones, time isn't literally his mouth, but seeing the Supreme within the powerful in this world assists our ability to focus the mind and facilitates meditation.

How many of us have contemplated the mystery of the sun and moon and our dependence on the light and warmth of the sun for our existence, or the movements of the moon and its effects on the weather and pull on water that so supports plant growth? The Gita provides all these hints for how we can perceive the Source of everything in the world around us, as "pearls are strung on an invisible thread."

I can choose to change my angle of vision from how the world can satisfy me to how I can satisfy my Source. Every time I see another, I perceive a soul, and sitting in the heart alongside that individual soul is the Great Soul, our collective Friend and shelter. As my vision clears and I see the presence of my Divine Other everywhere, my affection for him increases and my familial feelings with all others intensifies. As my affection for the Supreme Person increases, so does my devotion, and I begin to feel the space that still separates us. I want to see him with my own eyes, in front of me – and this longing continues to increase. Separation is a powerful emotion that nurtures love. It acts like a magnet drawing to us the person we desire to be with.

Sri Radha's "Song to the Bumblebee," related in the Bhagavata, is an amazing display of the intensity of love in separation. Called by his uncle, Krishna had moved from his rural home in Vrindavan to the city of Mathura. In his absence, maddened by separation in divine love, Radha was on the verge of death. Krishna knew of her condition, so he sent her a message through his intimate friend, Uddhava, who resembled Krishna in dress, age, and complexion. When Radha saw Uddhava she wept upon being reminded of her Krishna. She was so disoriented by her separation from Krishna that she couldn't hear Uddhava speaking to her. Distracted by love in separation, she imagined that a bumblebee humming around her at that moment bore a message from Krishna. Then, in the madness of separation, she spoke to the bee at length, revealing her innermost heart – in front of Uddhava, but completely unaware of his presence.

Uddhava was well acquainted with divine love since he possessed it himself and had seen it in the hearts of so many others. But he was stunned to witness the intensity and purity of Radha's love, which was unexcelled – he had never experienced such a depth of divine love. He bowed to her, saying, "I am indebted to you. How would I know about the deep truths of love in separation unless you showed them to me? Krishna has become your exclusive servant because you love him so intensely."

As mentioned earlier, in the company of others whose love is mature, our own love is coaxed out and nurtured. When we hear about Sri Radha's and Sri Chaitanya's feelings of separation from Krishna – or the feelings of other residents of the spiritual world – we witness the pure soul's condition when separated from its Source, who is an ocean of love. Without our Supreme Friend, the soul is inconsolable. We are inconsolable. We feel it even now but haven't yet been able to name it.

As an atomic spark of sentience, we're lonely without our Source, so we play with people, pets, and all sorts of toys to distract ourselves from our feeling of being incomplete. That hole inside us that we all feel – the dissatisfaction, the confusion, the fear, the anxiety, the depression, the self-sabotage, the never-ending search for happiness – is the smoldering of the fire of separation from our all-attractive Krishna. Once we recognize the existential issue underlying our malaise, we're impelled to act in ways to reconnect with our Friend.

The beauty of separation is that it quickly draws us into the company of the Beloved. We're not left in a state of existential loneliness forever. Our angst, expressed in prema-kirtan of the maha-mantra, calls out to our Divine Other, who responds unfailingly with love. Krishna says, "I am completely under the control of my devotees, as if I have no independence at all. My heart is fully captivated by my virtuous devotees, for I am their only beloved."

The Dawning of Divine Love

There's an east-facing window in the sacred room where I meditate every morning. It's a quiet, deep black outside when I begin my chanting. I treasure this time before dawn – it allows for calm focus on the Names. As time passes, when the background palette outside is first stroked shades of gray, I start to make out sky between the limbs of the majestic oak outside my window, and slowly, hints of blue are revealed. At the first blush of color, a bird begins its happy song. As the sky brightens into a clear blue, the horizon gradually embraces delicate yellows, and the landscape is plainly visible as more birds join the chorus. Then I know that it's only a short time before the yellows will burst brilliant, sometimes adding pinks or oranges at their borders, and the sun will beam forth with its full, enlightening face.

In the awakening of divine love there's a similar dawning as we rid ourselves of entrenched patterns and leave the false self for our fully realized spiritual identity. The rising of pure love clarifies our vision, sings of unprecedented possibilities, and propels us toward our final goal with great longing. The inner life unfolds its mystery and glory as we hold steadfast in embracing the maha-mantra.

Sri Nama comes from the transcendental plane and invokes all perfections because of its pure transcendental nature. Though at first it's quiet and dark inside, the Name gradually reveals everything as surely as the rising sun. The interior landscape becomes known to us, we leave behind the gloom and shadows of our dark material existence, and we joyously welcome the rising potential of our relationship with Krishna, the root of our existence.

There are eight stages in the development of love of God, which Rupa Goswami describes:

While continuously wandering throughout this material universe, one who is fortunate achieves the company of saints and imbibes from them (1) faith, or a preliminary trust, in the promise that the process will work. We then seek their (2) holy association and (3) take up bhakti activities under their tutelage. A daily spiritual practice (4) removes the obstacles on our path toward purification. When this work is completed, (5) our faith becomes firm and steady, and then we're quickly brought (6) to experience a taste, or the sweetness of bhakti, loving devotional service. (7) Then we develop a genuine attachment to our Beloved, the object of our love, (8) which matures into ecstatic feelings and then divine love ripens to its full sweetness. These are the stages toward prema, or divine love.

To enter our sacred interior in earnest we need faith or trust in the practice of bhakti, which we receive by hearing from and associating with persons experienced in the wonders of bhakti. This inspires us to try a practice of mantra meditation. If we stay in contact with helpful practitioners, we'll find ourselves willing to commit to our practice, and from there we'll begin to experience the milestones of progressive spirituality. With enthusiasm, patience, and determination, we'll find the mantra carrying us through the stages leading to the ultimate goal, prema.

If you've been engaged in the yoga of kirtan and have not experienced its power, then you can determine from the seven stages above where you are in the progressive development of bhakti. It can be that you're in early stages and will gain experience with more practice. And you can diagnose the slowness in your progress by carefully examining the motives behind your practice, reviewing your conceptual understanding of the Name, and considering the moods you embrace while chanting.

Rupa Goswami poetically describes his own encounter with the holy names:

I do not know how much nectar
the two syllables *krish* and *na* have produced.
When the holy name of Krishna is chanted
it appears to dance within the mouth.
We then desire many, many mouths.
When that name enters the holes of the ears
we desire many millions of ears.
And when the holy name
dances in the courtyard of the heart,
it conquers the activities of the mind,
and all the senses become inert.

Part III

THE UNIVERSE
OF KIRTAN

Chapter 9

THE ORIGINS
OF KIRTAN
& THE POWER
OF BHAKTI

*Bhakti is the very essence
of the ocean of immortality.*
– Narada

We've become somewhat acquainted with prema-kirtan and its practices but have heard little of its roots and development, including how kirtan came to us in the West.

In the Cradle of Civilization
Scholar-historian Guy Beck gives us a comprehensive overview of the history – from the ancient to the present – of sacred sound and music in India his books *Sonic Theology, Sacred Sound,* and *Sonic Liturgy.* We learn that in the world's oldest texts, kirtan was called *anukirtana. Anu* means both "following great saints" and "continuous," and refers to the recitation of a

mantra, prayer, hymn, or poem during various rituals in praise or glorification of a cosmic controller (deva) or the Godhead, who is the fountainhead of all forms of divinity. A person who possesses superior beauty, courage, knowledge, and is capable of superior action is usually remembered through kirtan.

At one point in our early history, chanting Vedic mantras was the private affair of highly trained (mostly) male priests, who intoned mantras and hymns, but it's doubted they had musical accompaniment.

The Vedas, the most ancient of Indian texts, where the mantras come from, refer to a number of divine personalities who play musical instruments. Saraswati, goddess of learning and music, strums a vina. Shiva, god of cosmic destruction, shakes a damaru drum. Brahma, god of the secondary creation, plays hand cymbals. Vishnu, the Oversoul, sounds a conch. Sri Krishna, who is known as the quintessential musician, plays a flute.

That the major divine personalities play instruments from all four classifications of instruments (as we know them today) – string, woodwind, brass, and percussion – may suggest that musical instruments are not a human invention. Regardless, music has always been sacred in Indian spirituality so it seems inevitable that eventually these early prayers and mantras would be set to music. When mantras and hymns were put to music, kirtan came to be known as chant accompanied by musical instruments. Kirtan is therefore thousands of years old.

Now, fast forward to the sixth century, when kirtan became publicly prominent in South India and then, gaining momentum, spread northward through the sixteenth century as if garlanding all of India.

The Alwar saint-poets of South India began the bhakti movement in the sixth century. They broke from institutionalized religious conventions and revitalized the bhakti tradition by demonstrating the vibrant life of a mystic's direct experience of the Divine. The Alwars wandered to temples and towns, singing their hymns of love for Vishnu and Krishna. Rising from the depths of the ancient traditions that had obscured the bhakti within them, these saints' example showed the joy of passionate devotion. Almost simultaneously, devotee-saints of Shiva, known as the Nayanars, added to the fervor of devotional love growing in the south.

The Alwars and Nayanars initiated the bhakti revival movement that challenged caste hierarchy, empty ritual, blind faith, and the notion that severe asceticism and renunciation (a mostly male enterprise) was the only way of attaining spiritual perfection. By singing in their vernacular rather than in Sanskrit – the language used for religious ceremonies and heady philosophical debates – they gave voice to the disenfranchised and permission to all people to express their heart in their own language. Their messages sought universal brotherhood and religious tolerance and inclusion. Sanskritist V. Raghavan calls bhakti "a democratic doctrine which consolidates all people without distinction of caste, community, nationality, or sex."

The saint-poets proved, through their kirtan and personal examples, that everyone has equal access to the divine, and they encouraged social reform, service, and charity; bhakti naturally encourages sacred activism because of its proposal to engage in the world with compassion and a detached service attitude while communing directly with the Supreme.

The universal appeal and practical application of bhakti was thus sparked, and the poem-songs of these saints, which are seen as the development of modern kirtan, spread so powerfully that it drowned out other messages and changed the face of South Indian history.

In his essay "The Nature and History of Hinduism," published in *The Religion of the Hindus,* D. S. Sarma writes, "Beside their [the Alwars' and Nayanars'] flaming devotion to God, their utter humility and self-surrender, and the joyousness of their religious experience, the atheistic creeds of Buddhism and Jainism shrank into cold and repulsive systems of self-torture. It has been truly said that the Alwars and Nayanars sang Buddhism and Jainism out of southern India."

Elsewhere in India, Tulsidas, Ramananda, Surdas, Tukaram, Meerabai, Guru Nanak, Namdev, Sri Chaitanya, Narottama, Bhaktivinoda Thakura, and others further contributed to bhakti poetry and song, and their influence reached out and touched those outside the kirtan traditions too. Kabir is a notable example; by many accounts, he was infatuated with Ramananda, the noted poet-saint who established a bhakti lineage called the Ramanandi sampradaya.

The goal of these poets' music was to produce a mystical love for the Divine; a spiritual emotion that could lead participants to liberation by gradually – and fully – absorbing the mind and heart in feelings for the Supreme. While accomplishing this elevated task, the music of kirtan also made life enjoyable. It's no wonder that the kirtan of these saints impacted people so deeply.

Especially noteworthy in the tradition is Jayadeva, a poetic genius whose epic poem, *Gita-Govinda,* about the love of Radha and Krishna, set a new standard for poetry and kirtan as well as Hindustani and Carnatic classical music. The poem inspired countless dramas, paintings, sculptures, musical compositions, and other pieces of art.

Not only is the *Gita-Govinda* considered the finest example of Sanskrit poetry, but the poem astounds theologians worldwide with the revelation that God subordinates himself to love. Krishna is conquered and completely controlled by Radha's pure love. Radha demonstrates love's ability to conquer the unconquerable, and by her example, she invites us into her divine dance of love.

Sri Chaitanya Mahaprabhu was absorbed in devotion to Radha and Krishna. Among all the saints of the bhakti renaissance, Sri Chaitanya's devotional ecstasies were unparalleled. Christian theologian John Moffit writes, "Of all the saints in recorded history, East or West, he seems to me the supreme example of a soul carried away on a tide of ecstatic love of God."

Though earlier saints had sung their own compositions, Mahaprabhu brought attention to the maha-mantra found in the Upanishads. It is not a product of someone's mind, but revealed sound that has unsurpassed power, being the sonic representation of the Supreme. In other words, maha-mantra kirtan is in a transcendent category unto itself.

Sri Chaitanya's kirtans were unlike all others because he brought kirtan to the streets as no other bhakti revivalist did. Thousands followed him. His kirtan uplifted the masses and reached further into the socio-religious framework than that of the Alwars and Nayanars. In his summary of *History of Bangla Kirtan,* by Hites Rajan Sanyal, Narasingha Sil is quoted, "Above all [the saint-poets of the bhakti movement], Chaitanya emerged as the leader of *bhakti-dharma* and the greatest proponent and popularizer of *samkirtan.*"

Even the king of Puri – who had seen countless mendicants,

ascetics, sages, and pilgrims from all over India coming to visit the famous Jagannatha temple in his city – had never seen this type of love of God manifest in kirtan before. His wonder is captured in Krishna Dasa Kaviraja's *Sri Chaitanya Charitamrita* (2.11.96–97): "I have never before seen such ecstatic love, nor heard the vibration of the holy name of the Lord chanted in such a way, nor seen such dancing during *kirtana*." His minister replied, "This sweet transcendental sound is a special creation of Sri Chaitanya known as *prema-kirtana*."

Kirtan Comes West

In April 1926, at New York City's Carnegie Hall, Paramahamsa Yogananda taught and led the singing of "O God Beautiful." He had translated the chant, written by Guru Nanak, into English, and was delighted how well the audience received it. It was sung in the style of classical music for an hour and a half. Though not sung in traditional kirtan style, there were some similarities.

It would be another forty years before New York City would become the first city in the Western world to welcome prema-kirtan. In 1966, A. C. Bhaktivedanta Swami sat down alone in Tompkins Square Park at the base of a now famous elm tree with a pair of Indian hand cymbals, karatals, and began to chant the Hare Krishna maha-mantra to whoever wanted to stop and listen.

Dubbed the "divine minstrel" by Philip Goldberg in his *American Veda,* Bhaktivedanta Swami went on to bring Sri Chaitanya's prema-kirtan to every continent, initiating a kirtan explosion in the West. His efforts revitalized the practice of prema-kirtan in India, too, and chanting the maha-mantra spread like wildfire all over the Indian subcontinent. It's now the primary kirtan heard there.

Besides being a minstrel, Bhaktivedanta Swami was also a Sanskrit scholar. In addition to his translation of the Bhagavad Gita he gave the English world his translations of the 18,000-verse *Srimad Bhagavatam* (Bhagavata) and the 11,000-verse *Chaitanya-charitamrita,* which garnered the attention of scholars around the world and nurtured the hearts of the devoted, growing the bhakti community into the millions. His literary contribution extolled the glory and power of sacred sound and bhakti as a doctrine and firmly established the philosophical basis of kirtan as the yoga practice *par excellence.*

Seeds of prema-kirtan were being sown elsewhere, too. Krishna Das and Jai Uttal, devotees of Neem Karoli Baba (the guru of Ram Dass of *Be Here Now* fame), who are now famous kirtan artists, were attracted to the prema-kirtan of the maha-mantra. Jai Uttal was initially drawn to the street kirtans of Bhaktivedanta Swami's followers but honed his musical expertise through lessons with Ali Akbar Khan. Krishna Das relates how Neem Karoli Baba would invite followers of Sri Chaitanya to his ashram to chant. That around-the-clock prema-kirtan of the Hare Krishna maha-mantra and the diverse melodies that those followers of Sri Chaitanya sang was the beginning of Krishna Das' attraction to kirtan.

While there are other excellent kirtan artists whose contact with kirtan came about in other ways, a strong argument can be made that Sri Chaitanya's prema-kirtan of the Hare Krishna maha-mantra is the primary genesis of kirtan in the West.

Five hundred and thirty-five years ago, Sri Chaitanya predicted that the kirtan of the Hare Krishna maha-mantra would spread all over the world. He foretold that prema-kirtan would send out waves of influence, touching souls in every culture far into the future because of its timelessness, universality, and capacity to heal hearts and transform lives. You and I find ourselves at a unique time in history as we witness the unfolding of his prophecy.

THE GOLD STANDARD OF ULTIMATE WEALTH

If rasa did not exist
in the sky of the heart,
who could inhale?
Who could exhale?
Verily, this rasa gives bliss.
– Taittiriya Upanishad 2.7

I have explained that the love-call to Sri Krishna is prema-kirtan, but I haven't discussed kirtans to Shiva, Durga, Ganesh, Laksmi, Sarasvati, Hanuman, or other personalities we hear about within the yoga traditions, or for that matter other divinities such as Buddha, Allah, Yahweh, or Jesus

Christ, Mohammed, and other saints and mystics from the world's various traditions. Are kirtans and songs to them also prema-kirtan?

The Gold Standard

In the *Taittiriya Upanishad* we learn that Brahman – which is the term used in the Upanishads to refer to the Supreme – is *raso vai sah*. *Rasa* means "unlimited spiritual emotions of ecstatic delight." The word *Brahman* can mean either the individual soul, the impersonal feature of the Absolute, or the Personal Absolute. Which Brahman does this text refer to? Who is full of unlimited ecstatic spiritual emotion thus making them the Supreme? By identifying the Supreme, we determine whose kirtan brings about prema, as rasa and prema are synonymous.

The statement *raso vai sah* tells us that we can identify Reality, the fountainhead of consciousness, by locating the one who experiences the greatest ecstasy and who has the fullest capacity to reciprocate love and experience its sublime, divine emotions.

Gold is the standard by which we judge the strength of a nation's currency; love is the standard by which we judge consciousness, or spirit.

B. R. Sridhar Goswami says that rasa (bliss/divine love) is the gold standard for consciousness. "No one can deny they want happiness. None will say that they won't avoid misery. All are common [as one] here: we are [each] searching for bliss. So the common standard of measurement is rasa. Blissfulness, beauty, charm, sweetness, love, affection – they all are of the same plane, and we cannot deny that we are all searching for that. This is everyone's inner necessity: rasa."

This makes rasa the standard by which we should measure all philosophies, theories, forms of spirituality, religions, other existential matters – and kirtans – because rasa is the nectar that attracts us, spirit-consciousness. And as rasa attracts us, it also attracts our Source, the Original Conscious Person. Love is the standard of excellence for both the finite self and the Infinite Self since both are feeling, conscious persons and it is love that attracts individuals.

Let's continue our search to unveil the supreme embodiment of rasa, and thereby identify prema-kirtan, by referring to Vyasa, the legendary author of the entire canon of Vedanta. He states that Truth is the nondual Supreme Consciousness. Vyasa's comprehensive perspective on Truth encompasses and harmonizes all the ways humans have conceived of the Supreme Reality as both immanent and transcendent, impersonal and personal. He explains that the Supreme is inconceivably personal and impersonal, immanent and transcendent *simultaneously.* Wouldn't the Supreme, by definition, encompass everything? Wouldn't the all-powerful be able to harmonize everything?

Vyasa describes that the nondual Absolute has three features based on three degrees of expression.

But wait, if the nondual were to express itself in various features wouldn't that mean it wasn't nondual, which is an impossibility for ultimate Reality?

That the Absolute Reality is nondual doesn't mean that nothing else exists. Rather, the word *nondual* means that the Absolute is self-existent (it's grounded in itself and depends on no external support), and nothing else exists *independent* of this nondual Reality's support.

The *Brihad-aranyaka Upanishad* (4.4.19) states, "The

Supreme is blissful, with no tinge of unhappiness. Although he is the oldest, he never ages, and although he is one, he is experienced in different forms."

Think of yourself. You're the same person even though you express yourself in one manner at work, in another way with your family, and in another with a close friend.

Similarly, the nondual Absolute expresses itself in three identifiable features corresponding to the characteristics of consciousness: being, knowing, and loving (*sat-chit-ananda*). Stated differently, Supreme Consciousness, although one Reality, takes on specific forms that showcase, or correspond with, or are phases of, each of the three intrinsic aspects of consciousness.

And these three features are variously understood according to how *we* approach the Supreme, which is why there are various definitions in the world of the same Supreme. In other words, Reality expresses itself in *three degrees of completion* in response to how we approach.

A. C. Bhaktivedanta Swami gave an example of three people who see a train for the first time. One person hears the whistle and sees the light of the distant train approaching at night then leaves and explains what a train is. The second person, waiting longer, makes out the engine and that many cars are part of the train, then excitedly leaves to describe the train. The third person remains on the platform until the train halts and sees passengers exiting. He approaches the person driving the train, shakes his hand, and asks him to explain everything about the train and then relays his experience to his friends. Each person accurately recounts their experience of the train, but some only have a partial view of it.

The list below may help you further conceptualize this in relationship to the Absolute.

Three Expressions of Consciousness: The Nondual Truth

1. Being, Sat
First realization of Truth

Brahman. The impersonal, all-pervading, illuminating, and ineffable is the Absolute without form or qualities, without distinctions of subject and object, and predominantly corresponds with the *being* – the "isness" – aspect of Consciousness.

Brahman realization entails perceiving a nature opposite of the mundane; it is a realization of the Supreme that is not manifesting all of its potencies.

Depending on the tradition, people may call their conception of Brahman as God, Allah, Yahweh, the Omnipresent, or a name in their tradition to name the Divine as impersonal.

Sri Jiva, a pre-eminent bhakti theologian, writes, "Just as the newborn babe perceives a manifold of sense which it cannot yet discriminate or assimilate or reduce to perception through the categories of the understanding, so the devotee in his state of trance is unable to appreciate the infinite excellence and perfection of the Lord's Personality and receives a vague distinctionless intuition in his soul." Some say perceiving Brahman is the first moment of the vision of the Absolute.

2. Knowing, Chit
Second realization of Truth

Paramatma. The immanent and transcendent, indwelling

Oversoul is the witness and inner tutor in every living being's heart. He is responsible for the cosmic order, including the creation and maintenance of the material worlds. He is known as the descending Absolute coming into this plane of existence. Paramatma predominantly corresponds with the *knowing* aspect of Consciousness.

Paramatma realization entails perceiving the Absolute as localized in the heart and immanent in the world. The Oversoul is a partial manifestation of the Supreme in the world.

Other names for Paramatma are God, Allah, Yahweh, Vishnu, Ishwara, Purusha, or the Omnipotent and Omniscient, depending on the tradition, when referring to the immanent God in the world and/or God situated in the heart of the living being along with the finite soul.

3. Loving, Ananda
Third realization of Truth

Bhagavan. The fully transcendent personal Absolute, who turns his full attention to the supra-cosmic sphere, corresponds with the *loving* feature of Consciousness.

Bhagavan realization entails perceiving the supramundane feature of the substantive Absolute in his self-manifest, original form as he is, free of all material conceptions and endowed with all transcendental potencies.

The generic epithet *Bhagavan* means "one who possesses all opulences" and refers to Sri Krishna. The epithet also refers to his innumerable personal expansions known as the Vishnus and Narayanas, who have various names such as Sri Rama, the Creator, etc.

Mystics of the various traditions who speak of a transcendental personality, or God, in the land beyond death are referring to one of these Vishnus or Narayanas, who have unlimited names and forms.

Sri Krishna, however, is Svayam Bhagavan ("Bhagavan himself"), or the original and complete Bhagavan. He is the source-Bhagavan. There is a difference between Sri Krishna and his expansions. The expansions emanate a commanding presence full of grand majesty. Because their opulence is infinite and the soul is exceedingly small, a mood of awe and reverence in the soul's approach to them is unavoidable.

In contrast, Sri Krishna hides his majesty, opulence, and immeasurability, and exhibits an approachable and relatable human*like* form to facilitate intimate loving exchanges with him. He is known as the supremely sweet manifestation of the Absolute by virtue of four distinctive *madhuris,* or sweetnesses, that *only* he possesses and to an unlimited degree. They are the beauty of his bodily form (*rupa-madhuri*); the enchanting sound of his mellifluous flute (*venu-madhuri*), the charm of his pure qualities (*guna-madhuri*), and the tenderness of his loving pastimes (*lila-madhuri*).

These three realizations or phases of the nondual substance, Absolute Reality, progress in degrees of completeness. We can understand how the loving feature of the Supreme is the most complete of its three features by logical deduction.

Anyone who loves (*ananda*) must exist (*sat*) and be cognizant (*chit*) – to love is to exist and to know. But someone who only exists doesn't necessarily know or love; someone who only exists and knows doesn't necessarily love. Therefore, the loving feature of consciousness is the most integral state, and the features of existence and cognizance are partial expressions of that whole.

Since a partial expression of something cannot, by definition, contain all the elements of the whole, it therefore cannot be the origin of the whole. By this logic, the loving feature of Supreme Consciousness is the Whole, and the other two features are partial expressions of the Whole.

This is explicitly stated in the Gita (15.18) where Krishna says,

yasmat ksharam atito 'ham
aksharad api chottamah
ato 'smi loke vede ca
prathitah purushottamah

Because I am superior to the *atmas* [individual souls], to the Brahman, and to the *purusha* known as Paramatma, and even to the other forms of Bhagavan, I am celebrated in the *Vedas* and the *smritis* as the Supreme Person.

With the understanding that the Absolute can manifest itself in a multitude of ways without being changed, let's continue our exploration of who is *raso vai sah*.

As we heard, Bhagavan, the Supreme Person, is the very form of ananda. Ananda ("bliss" or "ecstatic love") is synonymous with rasa ("unlimited spiritual emotions of ecstatic delight"); ananda is rasa. Therefore, Bhagavan is *raso vai sah*.

But there are other personalities in the yoga philosophies,

and kirtan is often performed in their names. Could any of them be *raso vai sah*? Let's make a comparative study.

For rasa to exist there must be a relationship. We experience that relationships are a primary force that impel action and give our lives meaning. Isn't almost everything we do driven by relationships with those we love, respect, or care for? So, too, on the metaphysical plane: relationships are the essence of our lives. Relationships in this mortal world are faulty, they are pale reflections of the pure relationships we can have in the divine domain. What types of spiritual relationships are available to us there?

We can stand at a distance in awe and reverence of the Complete Person, or we can become a close friend who doesn't want to let go of his hand even in dreams. Or we can become a doting elder who smothers him with protective affection, or we can become his intimate lover.

In other words, there are spiritual counterparts of the full variety of relationships that so engage and enthrall us in this world. If this were not so wouldn't spiritual existence be less than material existence? That is not possible. Thus the Supreme Person must, by definition, be able to share the full array of loving exchanges and accommodate the uniqueness of each soul who will be attracted to different moods. Therefore we can choose to engage in one of these relationships with the object of love being the Absolute. These relationships are powerful forces of paramount bliss in the absolute degree – rasa – for both the soul and the Infinite.

Let's consider the relationships that are possible to have with the various divinities to locate who is capable of extending the full expression of rasa, or prema.

Who is Raso Vai Sah?

Personality	Type of Relationship Possible
Impersonal One (Brahman or other impersonal conceptions)	none
Durga Devi (or other goddesses of this world)	passive adoration; master-servant; mother-child (the soul can only be in the servant or child position in relationship to the universal mother)
Lord Shiva (or other demigods and cosmic administrators of this world)	passive adoration; master-servant (the soul can only be in the servant position)
Paramatma (Immanent God, Allah, Yahweh, Vishnu, Purusha, Ishwara)	passive adoration; master-servant (the soul is in the servant position)
Bhagavan Vishnus and Narayanas (Transcendent God, Allah, Yahweh, Vishnu, Narayana, Sri Rama)	passive adoration; master-servant (the soul is in the servant position)
Svayam Bhagavan Sri Krishna	passive adoration; master-servant; friend-friend; child-parent (the soul can be either parent or child according to the nature of the love felt); lover-Beloved

As we compare possibilities, we find that Sri Krishna recip-rocates all the varieties of loving exchanges. He is therefore known as *akhila-rasamrita-murti,* "the embodiment of the ambrosia of immortal joy known as rasa," and *Rasa Raj,* "the king of rasa."

In this way, Krishna is the heart of divinity itself; he is the full expression of Brahman, the sweet Supreme, who is *raso vai sah.*

The human body is similar in shape and structure to Sri Krishna's body, but the "ingredients" of Krishna's body are not material. His body is not made of "stuff" different from him; his body is made of condensed existence, knowledge, and bliss. Unlike us, he and his body are identical. Both are spirit, and just as his name is identical with him, so too is his body, due to the nature of the nonduality of spirit.

In *Vaisnava Vedanta,* Mahanamabrata Brahmachari writes, "As water becomes ice due to excessive cold so does the abso-lute consciousness assume a form due to the exuberance of joy and delight.... His body is nothing but pure consciousness and joy condensed. The Absolute has got no limbs like ours which are made up of the five sensuous elements, but really possesses supersensuous limbs of which the sole ingredient is bliss and consciousness."

What can't be shown in the chart is the *measure* of rasa in Bhagavan Sri Krishna, who is an infinitely expanding embodi-ment of divine love – there is no limit to Krishna. In both scope and depth, the rasa in Sri Krishna's divine play is without equal. We can learn about Krishna's sweet personality and the extent of his genuine love and loving affairs in the Bhagavata Purana. There we find that the soul has the greatest opportu-nity to share love with the Divine.

We've learned that rasa is the experience of transcendental, ecstatic emotional states, arising from personal exchanges with Love Personified. But it's not a one-way love. Rasa is a mutual reciprocation of affection. The soul experiences and relishes rasa, and the Source Soul, Sri Krishna, experiences and relishes rasa. In the reciprocal exchange of love each tries to outdo the other – neither ever fully succeeding, but each continuing to try – which makes divine love ever-fresh and ever-expanding at every step, eternally. In these ways prema is completely different from mundane love.

The same *raso vai sah* Upanishadic verse continues, "One who obtains this rasa becomes blissful" (*rasam hy evayam labdhvanandi bhavati*).

There is no happiness greater than the bliss awarded by kirtan for Krishna, which nourishes the natural attraction the soul has for its Source Soul – its ground of being. And maha-mantra meditation prepares us and welcomes us to the full variety of loving exchanges with the Absolute. Thus kirtan for raso vai sah Sri Krishna is prema-kirtan.

Let's look at one more comparative study, using the hints we've received from sacred texts about who is Supreme among the many forms of divinity.

Within the Vedic pantheon of gods and goddesses, we find that each has a duty to perform. Brahma, the universal architect, is busy looking in all directions to manage the creation. Durga rides a tiger, weapons in each of her ten hands, tasked with keeping evil forces in check. Shiva is responsible for universal destruction. While waiting to do his duty, he spends his time in meditation on his source. Vishnu, the transcendental Supreme Controller (whose other names are Ishwara, Purusha, God, Yahweh, or Allah), is the maintainer of the universe and is always on call. Paramatma, the immanent Oversoul, attentively sees to the needs of each being and dispenses its karma. All of these superior personalities have functions in the world of matter. Those who have duties to perform are not independent; they are acting on someone else's behalf.*

This is not so for Sri Krishna who delegates all duties to others. The *Taittiriya Upanishad* (2.8.1) states, "Out of fear of him, the wind blows. Out of fear of him, the sun moves, and Agni and Indra execute their duties. And death, the fifth of their number, races along out of fear of him."

Neither does Krishna have duties in the spiritual realm. Rather, he plays – always. He isn't in search of perfection; he has no duty. He is always shown playing a flute and frolicking carefree in the natural settings of his abode.

The depictions we find of each of these many personalities carry a message: the one who is only playing is the all-powerful one. Those who wish to spend their time in play necessarily have power; to always play, one must have *all* power. The only divine person that fits this description is Sri Krishna.

In addition to his unmatched skill as a flautist, Krishna is known for his expertise in singing and dancing, so he naturally loves to hear kirtan. It's interesting to note that of all the divinities, only Sri Krishna specifically asks for kirtan.

---

* For a fuller discussion of avatars, shaktis, expansions, and representatives of the Supreme and to make sense of the complex yoga universe, see the QR code at the beginning of the appendix.

Chapter 11

COSMIC JOURNEYS

What Sri Chaitanya Mahaprabhu revealed
through the practice of maha-mantra yoga
is no less than a means of gaining access
to the very realm where that ultimate embodiment
of infinite existence, knowledge, and bliss resides and relates.
That transcendent sphere of consciousness existing
far beyond the enormity of this universe is our true home.
As atomic specks of consciousness, we belong there.
– Richard Whitehurst

We're far more powerful than we've been led to believe; we're immeasurably more than what meets the eye. In choosing a mantra to dedicate yourself to, you choose among a vast array of possibilities for the soul – one more enchanting and enthralling than any you've encountered in any wonderful dream or fictional world. If you focus on the spiritual practice of mantra meditation, you can choose where to go and who you'll be in eternity.

It's a profound awakening to realize that meditating on a particular mantra makes you an empowered agent of your own destiny and gives you access to higher realms and higher versions of yourself. Our spiritual prospects aren't limited, nor are limits dictated to us by others.

Mantras act like vehicles that can carry us somewhere after we leave behind our current mind-body at death. Where do you want to go? Answering this question will help you choose your mantra and kirtan accordingly. Which kirtans do you *want* to hear?

The atma can:

1. remain in the earthly realm
2. enter the celestial regions above the earth
3. enter the intermediary region between matter and spirit, which is the abode of Shiva and Parvati
4. merge into featureless, impersonal oneness (Brahman)
5. enter Vaikuntha, a spiritual realm where unlimited forms of the Supreme Person reside (Narayana, Vishnus, Allah, God, Yahweh, etc.)
6. enter Maha-Vaikuntha, Goloka, the plane of existence on which all other destinations rest – the abode of Svayam Bhagavan Sri Krishna

Here on Earth

Since our interest lies in mantra meditation for spiritual attainment, we can set aside the goal of staying on earth. We don't need to do anything different in our lives to return to the earth in our next birth, though it's important to note that the yoga philosophies explain that in the earthly sphere, we cycle through all the different life forms. That is, we don't always have the good fortune to be reborn as humans. A human birth is a rare and extremely valuable attainment because it gives us the option to evolve and expand our consciousness.

Celestial Region

The celestial realms are within the material creation, and the level of pleasure and the lessening of suffering in those regions is the reward for good karmic acts. While these heavenly pleasures far surpass those available on earth, these realms are still temporary places where, after residing for a long period, we return to the earthly region for further karmic cycling.

Vedic cosmography refers to the celestial regions as Swarga, a "world of light and devas." These "upper planets" are home to Brahma (of the triad of universal gods: Brahma, Shiva, and Vishnu), and cosmic administrators (devas) like Indra, Vayu, Agni, Surya, as well as highly accomplished yogis and sages.

One becomes qualified to receive a passport for travel there – by chanting the mantras or names of Shiva, Durga, Rama, the Vishnus, or Krishna, each of whom is capable of stamping their devotees' passports with visas and allowing them to reside anywhere in the celestial realms. This is not, however, liberation from the material world but a destination within the material cosmos: the soul remains entrapped in matter.

Intermediary Region

Beyond the celestial regions we find Shiva's abode, which sits in an intermediate position between the material and spiritual regions. It's an eternal residence: although it's on the border between the two energies, it is, itself, spiritual. Those devoted to Shiva can choose to live here to be with and serve him. Chanting mantras and kirtans dedicated to Shiva, Durga,

Rama, the Vishnus, or Krishna can grant entry here, if those kirtans are infused with genuine bhakti.

The All-Pervasive

We can realize Brahman – all-pervasive, featureless, passive, nondynamic consciousness – by the blessings of the Supreme Person, because Brahman is his personal aura, or the effulgence that shines from his body. Vedanta explains that the soul must have a measure of bhakti for Krishna or Vishnu to be allowed to live in that light because the light is part of his body.

Mantras dedicated to Vishnu and Krishna have the ultimate discretion to open this facility to souls who desire it. It's unusual, though, for those who know the identity of Rama, Vishnu, or Krishna to aspire for this type of liberation, because most enjoy a personal relationship with one of these divinities and would not want to give that up. When the soul merges into Brahman, its individuality is suppressed along with the potential to have any relationship.

There's a common idea that the soul can merge into the oneness of Brahman by worshiping Shiva or Durga and chanting mantras dedicated to them. This is because, they say, Shiva and Durga are nondifferent from Brahman; they are Brahman in a personal, but temporary form. The soul can merge into Brahman because the soul is also nondifferent from Brahman. We are all one. There is no individual identity of the soul.

Worship of Shiva or Durga and chanting mantras and kirtan dedicated to them may grant this liberation from matter *if* the aspirant has some measure of genuine bhakti for Vishnu or Krishna, from whom Shiva and Durga derive their powers.

Going to this eternal, spiritual region is liberation from matter, or mukti. Once here, the soul remains forever in a state of peaceful repose, disembodied, devoid of identity and relationships and any other state that requires differentiating between one thing and another. This sameness means, in essence, that the soul enters a deep, sleeplike trance. No prema is found here because within featureless cognizance there is no emotion, no other to love, no sense of identity to differentiate oneself from any other being or thing.

Chanter Beware

Let's pause for a moment before speaking about the two final destinations. Savvy spiritual seekers should be aware of the following considerations.

When we engage in kirtan with a desire for fame, following, wealth, sex, or other types of personal gratification, and at the same time we don't fully engage with the knowledge and practices that can rid the heart of those impurities, then we're simply engaged in making mundane music. It may look like kirtan on the outside, but that "kirtan," even if using the maha-mantra, does not grant prema or mukti: it cannot liberate the lead singer(s) or those who hear them. In fact, it entangles one further in material existence.

Now, what about kirtans performed with a desire for liberation or to merge into Brahman? They are mukti kirtans, not prema kirtans – even if they use the maha-mantra. It is common for those who aim to merge into the impersonal, featureless One to use the mantras and worship of a personal divinity to facilitate their meditation practice, because it's nearly impossible – if not impossible – to meditate on nothing. What do you focus on during your meditation? What do you say or think about *nothing*? Certainly there's nothing in nothing to sing about. So those who aspire for nothingness use the mantra (and the person of the mantra) as a prop to aid them as they practice meditation. In the end such persons dispose of both the mantra and the divine person in the mantra.

I say "dispose of" because often such people consider Krishna, Rama, Vishnu, Shiva, and Durga inferior, temporary manifestations of the Supreme Brahman, sometimes even considering their forms material. They think that the mantras dedicated to them are means to a higher end; worship of their forms is simply helpful as they try to move from mind-body embodiment to material unembodiment. In this way they step on and over the names and personalities of the divine mantras, exploiting them for their own purposes.

Self-interest is a low expression of bhakti if it can even be called bhakti at all. By the neglect of both the mantra and the person in the mantra typical of self-interest, the glory and power of the Names is lost to the chanter (and those who hear their kirtans) and the divine person offended. Though these worshipers take the names "Rama," "Shiva," "Krishna," "Durga," "Hanuman," or "Ganesh," their chanting is devoid of pure bhakti. Kirtan performed with this conceptual orientation to the mantra and the Absolute may – possibly, if some bhakti is present – award mukti but never prema.

Kirtan by a person who believes the Names are mythical, material, or temporary, or who misunderstands the full import of the Names (even if the singer is chanting mantras that normally would have the power to grant prema) will be imbued with the incorrect conceptual understanding of the chanter and those who hear that kirtan will also be affected. Even ordinary music is infused with the conceptions of the composer and singer, and these are conveyed to listeners, who imbibe the same mood and understanding. In a similar way, one's consciousness will be imbued with the faulty, impure conception of such a lead chanter.

When we come to understand these distinctions, we can choose which kirtans to participate in and listen to. These are more important considerations than who has a pleasing voice, a magnetic personality, or musical talent.

Vaikuntha

The Vaikunthas are spiritual planets above Shiva's abode where the multitude of Vishnu forms, including Narayana, Rama, and other expansions of the Supreme Person, live along with their consorts: Lakshmi with Vishnu, Sita with Rama, or other complementary shakti expansions of the supreme goddess.

A significant difference between Vaikuntha and the material world is that the material world (the lower order) is cyclic, with evolution followed by degeneration. Vaikuntha (the higher order) is rectilinear (moving in a straight line); it moves on and on, ever increasing through eternity due to being a primary expression of the power of the Supreme Absolute. The material world is an expression of the secondary energy of the Absolute.

In the last chapter we heard that when other traditions speak of a transcendental place, they often refer (vaguely) to this spiritual realm. Those who are supremely devoted to the forms that the Supreme Person manifests in the transcendental realm live there on one of those planets with their lord and master.

Kuntha in the word *Vaikuntha* means "relief." In the material world, everyone is afraid of loss. Things are taken from us constantly – by time and ultimately by death. Many of us fear individuality in transcendence because of the disharmony we witness in ourselves and others in this world. Vaikuntha, however, is a world of dynamic unity – harmonious the way music is harmonious. We may think that unity requires that we all play the same note – or play no notes at all; but in Vaikuntha many notes play together, harmonized by the shared center of each soul: pleasing the all-attractive Supreme Person. We're familiar with the difference between the sound of one note and the harmony of an exquisite symphony produced by a musical genius. Such an attractive harmony gives joy to the ears and hearts of everyone.

Each of us is also faced with what feels like an ultimate loss of self – we fear death. But this fear, too, is nonexistent in Vaikuntha. There is nothing to lose because there is no death of the soul. Therefore no one you love will be lost to you, and all loving exchanges are therefore safe. So Vaikuntha facilitates ecstasy – the bliss of the *sat-chit-ananda* nature of spirit, and this is much more relishable than the soul's comalike state in Brahman. The happiness of Vaikuntha is so welcoming that just by arriving there one feels suddenly free of all fear.

Vaikuntha is a trans-space-and-time location, a transcendental dynamic plane. Bewilderment and delusion cease to exist. Ignorance and the inability to see Reality are removed. There is no aging; you remain forever youthful because to be so is the nature of the soul. And love pervades.

Imagine a place where everyone accepts you completely and wants to make you happy. How relaxed would you feel? You'd have no fear of harm, being exploited, misunderstood, betrayed, or in any way losing anything. In Vaikuntha all the residents are respectful because they see you in relation to the Supreme. The spiritual world is the land of giving, the land of love.

Such a place is beyond our imagining because we have no experience of such an environment. In this world we need to be careful what we say, how we say it, and to whom we say it. When someone comes to see us, we tend to want to protect ourselves from misunderstanding or some type of exploitation or loss. But in the spiritual world everyone loves everyone else. Therefore Vaikuntha is known as the realm of auspiciousness, immortality, and fearlessness.

The four Kumaras were sober, learned adepts of the yoga wisdom path, who considered Brahman, impersonal oneness, the highest, most desirable attainment. They were fully Brahman-realized and fixed in their purpose. On one journey, traveling by the power of their mystic yoga practice, they reached the border of Vaikuntha, beyond the celestial vault of matter. Just coming into Vaikuntha's proximity they found themselves overcome with ecstasy.

The Kumaras weren't allowed to enter because they lacked bhakti qualifications and so were turned away. But just by seeing the spiritual realm and meeting Bhagavan at the gates, they were inspired to glorify Vaikuntha and Vishnu with their full hearts and, developing a desire to go there, they abandoned their desire for the impersonal Brahman and fully embraced the bhakti path. In other words, divine love began to manifest in their hearts. Such is the charming power of the personal Absolute and the land beyond death.

If the Supreme's abode is so alluring, imagine the attractiveness of the person who created it!

Purely chanting the names of Vishnu or Krishna can grant residence here. We enter into an eternal life of prema, divine love as a state of being.

Here, finally – out of all the cosmic destinations – we find pure love. It is, however, love overcome by the supreme majesty of God, the omnipotent, omniscient, and omnipresent. In

Vaikuntha, then, prema is restrained by the residents' sense of awe and reverence for the Supreme, who is always seen as the master worthy of veneration. Awe and reverence naturally constrain intimacy: there remains a perpetual distance between the Supreme and the soul as the Infinite and the finite. The dutiful prema here, therefore, is tinged with reservation.

As we saw in the "Who is *Raso Vai Sah?*" chart in the previous chapter, one can have a relationship with the Supreme Person in this region only in the mood of a servant as we see in the relationship between Hanuman and Rama.

We've come a long way to find divine love, which demonstrates it is no small attainment. Therefore, those serious to attain it must carefully search it out and pursue it by attentive choice of their mantra meditation. It is the highest of the high.

Now, if we want, we can experience more intimacy with our Beloved. If we choose, we can go higher!

Goloka

Maha-Vaikuntha, also known as Goloka, is the highest of high worlds, the place of Sri Krishna and Sri Radha. The Divine Dyad are the full face of the Absolute in their original self-manifest forms. They are one, separated into two to taste the ambrosia of mutual love.

This domain revels in fully manifested divinity; the deepest mysteries of the universe flourish here; it's the principal residence of universal opulence including pure happiness and never-ending bliss. The Vaikunthas are merely a fractal portion of this sphere. Goloka is the embodiment of eternal truth and everything there is jewellike, being made of desire-fulfilling touchstones.

In Goloka, prema is fully expressed and we find the zenith

of spiritual intimacy with the Godhead. We can have a relationship with Krishna as servant, friend, parent, or lover. These very intimate relationships are possible because Krishna's supremacy is hidden by his original, causeless human*like* form – a form so beautiful and approachable that the residents can express their love freely, with the greatest intimacy. All distance between the finite and the Infinite is removed, and the soul and the Infinite become best friends or the most intimate lovers. In Goloka, Krishna becomes the dependent child of his adoring parents and elders, who sometimes correct him and always look to his welfare.

Just as a famous person likes to relax and act freely with friends and family, leaving aside all pretense or disguise, so Krishna relishes relationships in the private atmosphere of his absolute abode, where he is deeply loved and loves all others in even greater measure. He is not loved because he's the Supreme Controller full of all six opulences, greater than Narayana and all the Vishnus, or the Soul of all souls, but because he is the embodiment of all beauty and charm.

The supreme extent of divine love is that Krishna, the crest jewel of lovers, cannot give up his innate characteristic to come under the control of his beloved devotees; he accepts their mastery over him with great affection and submits to them completely. His happiness lies in their happiness; he is conquered and captured by divine love.

It's described that when Krishna looks at someone in Goloka, that person feels happy, but when that someone looks at him, he or she feels ten thousand times happier. Krishna gives others more joy than he derives from them because Krishna is joy personified! He is Infinite, and we are finite; he's unlimited, and we're atomic. How much joy can we give him? How much can the Infinite reciprocate with us? He's the unlimited source of ananda-rasa. If he wants to give joy, how much can we accept? This is why his devotees fall into unmatched trance ecstatic states. Krishna gives so much joy to his devotees that they become wild to serve him and be with him.

Krishna himself says, "Knowing my opulences, the whole world looks upon me with awe and veneration. But devotion made feeble by such reverence does not attract me." And later, "O Uddhava, pursuits such as the eight-step yoga, knowledge of oneself as one with Brahman, religiosity, Vedic study, all kinds of austerity, and selflessness in asceticism – none of these can bind me as intense devotion does. I can be reached only by devotional love born of unalloyed faith."

Such is the power of pure love. The divine play of rasa, or emotional exchanges with Krishna, is without limit. The bhakti texts give us details about the activities and psychology of the Supreme Person drawing our heart closer by getting to know the person named Krishna.

Rupa Goswami cautions, "My dear friend, if you are indeed attached to your worldly friends, do not look at the smiling face of Krishna as he stands on the bank of the Yamuna River. Casting charming, sidelong glances, he places his flute to his lips, which seem like delicate new blossoms. His transcendental body, bending in three places, appears very bright and attractive in the moonlight."

One who sees the source of truth, beauty, and harmony is overcome with love and loses interest in worldly affairs. For those who are attached to their bodies and material desires, this is an unwelcome result of contact with the Divine. And those who aspire to merge into the impersonal Brahman should not look at Krishna, because he is so alluring that they'll lose interest in their allegiance to the all-pervasive featureless One as did the Kumaras as they approached the border of Vaikuntha.

To enter Goloka, we require certain qualifications. No disturbing elements are allowed in. Each aspirant lives absorbed in prema – divine love as a state of being. Krishna and Radha grant entry to those who have qualified themselves through prema-kirtan of their holy names.

The intimacy of love in Goloka offers the richest options of love in transcendence – the greatest possibilities for the soul. Prema-kirtan takes us there on the happy wave of sacred sound to give us our highest prospect, a spiritual body and position in the world of love and beauty. In kindness to us, the process is very generous and easy. All we have to do is cooperate with the divine sound. Just chant and be happy – and then soar. You will, one day, feel the touch of your Divine Friend's hand in yours as you walk together into his transcendental town.

Welcomed Home

The *Brihad-Bhagavatamrita* offers a first-person account of Sarupa. After becoming free of his gross and subtle bodies, Sarupa attains a transcendental body and is transferred to Goloka.

On opening his eyes there, he is overwhelmed. Goloka is full of eternity, knowledge, and bliss, and endowed with form, taste, fragrance, touch, and sound in their full spiritual nature. He understands that what he is seeing has been made visible to him because Krishna drew back the curtain, revealing a wonderful picture. Sarupa says:

> I saw, by the hundreds of thousands and tens of millions,
> all sorts of wonders, unseen, uncommon, unimaginable

by anyone. I heard singing, and laughter, and a commotion at a distance. Then I heard from afar a certain sound. It was the supremely attractive murmur of Krishna's enchanting flute. That sound – sweet melodies of sportingly played notes, diverse with musical embellishments – was like nothing ever heard in the material world.

Then from a distance I saw Krishna with his charming flute in hand. Running quickly, he emerged from among his friends and approached me, saying in a sweet voice, "Look! Here is my dear friend Sarupa, the sun who shines on the lotus of my family!"

Krishna was dressed for the forest, where he always sports with his friends. His garments, earrings, and peacock-feather crown all swayed to and fro, and so did his garland of *kadamba* flowers. The fragrance of his transcendental body perfumed all directions, and his beautiful lotus face blossomed with a playful smile. His lotus eyes beamed with a merciful glance, and the varied assets of beauty decorated him in a singular way.

The fingers of his lotus hand busily pushed back the locks of his black hair, which flew about, adorned with the dust raised by the cows that he and his friends were herding. His tender, divine lotus feet touched the surface of the earth. Playfully dancing as they moved, they attracted everyone's heart with their great eagerness to walk quickly with large steps. The effulgence of his cloud-colored body, shining with the full sweetness of youth, lit up all corners of the sky. His beauty, which captured the hearts of the ever-dear devotees of Goloka, was an ocean abounding with countless excellences.

He came close to me, compelled by affection for me, his helpless devotee. I fainted in love upon seeing him and he caught hold of me. Then, suddenly he too fell to the ground. A moment later I awoke and as I stood up, I saw him lying unconscious on the ground, which he was moistening with his tears. Great numbers of birds, flying overhead, told of their misery by making a tumultuous noise that sounded like people crying. I was drowning in a vast ocean of sorrow seeing Krishna on the ground crying. Confused about what to do and severely tormented, I held Krishna's lotus feet and began profusely sobbing.

Krishna's elder brother Balarama, that most skillful of persons, made me hold his younger brother with my arms and call out to Krishna with many plaintive cries of his names. Then Balarama made me lift Krishna up from the ground. Suddenly Krishna opened his eyes, sealed till then by a flood of tears. Seeing me, he joyfully embraced and kissed me.

That best of Lords took my hand in his own – his own left hand – and received me as a long-lost bosom friend. He asked me, "Dear friend, are you healthy and happy? I have waited a long time for you."

Then he joyfully entered the best of cowherd villages with me by his side.

NOTE FROM THE AUTHOR

Thank you for reading *Prema Kirtan: Journey into Sacred Sound*.

If you were benefitted, it would be greatly appreciated if you left a review on Amazon, Goodreads, and other online sites so others can receive similar value by reading *Prema Kirtan*. Honest reviews help readers find books they're looking for. And reviews educate writers about what readers like. I read every review and take them to heart. I hope you can find a few minutes to tell us about your experience in reading *Prema Kirtan*.

As a thank you, please accept a gift of a free copy of *The Inner Loving Self,* which you can download at www.exploringbhakti.com.

APPENDIXES

PREMA KIRTAN EXTRAS

pranadacomtois.com/prema-kirtan-extras
exploringbhakti.com/prema-kirtan-extras

- Listen to the pronunciation of the maha-mantra
- Listen to different prema kirtans
- Listen to the "The Ecstasy of Separation" poem in these appendixes recited
- Read and listen to prema mantras
- A list of books for reading kirtan
- An essay on expansions, shaktis, avataras, and representatives
- Comments on the *Shikshashtaka* of Sri Chaitanya Mahaprabhu
- A video instruction on How to use a Bead Mala

THE ECSTASY OF
SEPARATION

The following is a found poem* from Sri Chaitanya's biography
Sri Chaitanya-charitamrita (3.14.41–54), by Krishna Dasa Kaviraja Goswami. Sri Chaitanya floated on the waves of blissful
kirtan each day, and in the evenings revealed his mind to his
close associates, often speaking like a madman in his separation
from Krishna.

Sri Chaitanya said,

My mind somehow achieved
the unmatched treasure, Krishna
but it lost him again.

In lamentation
my mind gave up my body,
abandoned all hope of material enjoyment,
and wandered as a yogi
with a skull for a begging bowl.

---

* A found poem is a prose text or texts reshaped by a poet into quasi-metrical
lines. In this found poem, I made some edits to the original text for brevity
and clarity, careful to retain the original meaning. For example, in the second
stanza I omitted the words *"kapalika* yogi" found in the original and replaced it
with a most notable characteristic of *kapalika* yogis: they use a human skull as a
begging bowl.

With immense desire to taste
Krishna's sweetness
my mind took its disciples, my senses,
to Vrindavan.*
It has given up proper behavior,
having lost its acquired gem.

O friends!
Where is my Lord Hari?†
Where is Hari?

The ring of Krishna's *rasa-lila*‡
is as pure as an earring made from a conch.§
The yogi of my mind wears that ornament.
From a gourd he has carved
the bowl of my aspirations
and taken the bag of my expectations
on his shoulder.

The yogi of my mind wraps the torn quilt
of anxiety around his body,
covered with dust and ashes.
His only words are *Alas! Krishna!*

---

* Krishna's home on earth – a replica of his abode in the spiritual sky. Vrindavan
  is known as Goloka in the spiritual sky.
† *Hari* is another name for Krishna.
‡ Krishna's circle dance of divine love with his transcendental sweethearts,
  the *gopis,* who are maidens who live in Goloka and are selflessly dedicated to
  Krishna in pure love. All atmas are invited into this dance when they engage in
  pure prema-kirtan.
§ Conch shells are considered pure in Vedic culture.

He wears twelve bangles of distress
and a turban of greed.
Because he has not eaten
he is very thin.

He always studies
the poetry about Krishna's Vrindavan *lila*[*]
by saintly yogis like Vyasa and Shuka,
who know Krishna as the Supreme Soul
beyond all contamination.

Taking all his disciples, my mind
begs door to door
from people and then
from the trees and creepers.

In Vrindavan
the *gopis* always taste
the nectar of Krishna's
sweetness and beauty,
the sound of his flute,
and the touch of his body.

The five disciples[†]
gather the remnants
of the *gopis'* nectar,
bringing them to the yogi of my mind.

---

[*] *Lila* means transcendental pleasure pastimes.
[†] The five disciples are the five senses.

Guru and disciples maintain their lives
by eating those remnants.

In one corner of a pavilion
in a solitary garden –
where Krishna enjoys his diversions –
the yogi of my mind and his disciples
practice mystic yoga. Wanting to see Krishna directly
they remain awake throughout the night
meditating on Krishna
who is unconstrained by the three ropes of matter.*

When my mind lost Krishna's company
and could no longer see him
it became depressed.

In that void my mind experienced
ten transformations.†
Agitated by these changes
my mind fled my body –
he left his place of residence empty –
and thus I am completely lost in trance.

---

* The three *gunas,* or "ropes," are *sattva* (illumination/goodness), *rajas* (confusion/
  passion), and *tamas* (darkness/inertia).
† The ten transcendental bodily transformations resulting from separation from
  Krishna when pure love manifests are anxiety, wakefulness, mental agitation,
  thinness, uncleanliness, talking like a madman, disease, madness, illusion, and
  near death. Sri Chaitanya was overwhelmed night and day by such ecstasies.
  Whenever the symptoms arose, his mind became unsteady.

Shikshashtaka

by Sri Chaitanya Mahaprabhu
translation by A. C. Bhaktivedanta Swami

In his youth, Sri Chaitanya was known as the most erudite scholar in Navadwipa, which rivaled the famous Benares (Varanasi) as a hub for intellectual giants. Despite his scholarship and renown as a teacher, he wrote almost nothing. Instead, his teachings were passed on through the writings of his direct disciples. But attributed to him is the *Shikshashtaka*. *Shiksha* means "instruction" and *ashtaka* means "eight." Hence the *Shikshashtaka* is a poem of eight stanzas, and they contain the essence of instruction on maha-mantra yoga.

Shikshashtaka

1

Let there be all victory for the chanting of the holy name of Sri Krishna, which can cleanse the mirror of the heart and stop the miseries of the blazing fire of material existence. That chanting is the waxing moon that spreads the white lotus of good fortune for all living entities. It is the life and soul of all education. The chanting of the holy name of Krishna expands the blissful ocean of transcendental life. It gives a cooling effect to everyone and enables one to taste full nectar at every step.

2

In your holy name there is all good fortune for the living entity, and therefore you have many names, such as "Krishna" and "Govinda," by which you expand yourself. You have invested all your potencies in those names, and there are no hard and fast rules for remembering them. Although you bestow such mercy upon the fallen, conditioned souls by liberally teaching your holy names, I am so unfortunate that I commit offenses while chanting the holy name, and therefore I do not achieve attachment for chanting.

3

One who thinks himself lower than the grass, who is more tolerant than a tree, and who does not expect personal honor but is always prepared to give all respect to others can very easily always chant the holy name of the Lord.

4

O Lord of the universe, I do not desire material wealth, materialistic followers, a beautiful wife or fruitive activities described in flowery language. All I want, life after life, is unmotivated devotional service to you.

5

O Krishna, son of Maharaja Nanda, I am your eternal servant, but because of my own fruitive acts I have fallen into this horrible ocean of nescience. Now please be causelessly merciful to me. Consider me a particle of dust at your lotus feet.

6

When will my eyes be beautified by filling with tears that constantly glide down as I chant your holy name? When will my voice falter and all the hairs on my body stand erect in transcendental happiness as I chant your holy name?

7

O Govinda, because of separation from you, I consider even a moment a great millennium. Tears flow from my eyes like torrents of rain, and I see the entire world as void.

8

Let Krishna tightly embrace this maidservant who has fallen at his lotus feet, or let him trample me or break my heart by never being visible to me. He is a debauchee, after all, and can do whatever me likes, but still he alone, and no one else, is the worshipable Lord of my heart.

CARE IN CHANTING

An essential aspect of the yogic science of mantra meditation is to avoid offenses to the Name. If we displease the Name, who is nondifferent from the person who is the Name, we can chant for a long time without much result. There are ten possible errors, called *aparadhas,* in Sanskrit, or "offenses," that we can make.

These offenses can be divided into two types. We can inadvertently offend the Name if we don't know enough about the characteristics of the Name and the Person of the mantra. I've laid out the proper conceptual orientation of the Name according to Bhakti Vedanta texts in *Prema Kirtan,* so if you're guided by this book, you won't fall prey to the offenses caused by simple ignorance.

The other category comes from contamination in the heart. For instance, the first offense is to criticize other chanters. Human beings have a general tendency to find fault with others, but Krishna doesn't take kindly to us if we criticize people working to purify themselves. Krishna dearly loves those who are dedicated to him. In other words, there is an intimate relationship between the Name, Krishna, and those who chant the Name. Criticism of saintly people – and anyone seriously attempting to love God is saintly, even if they are not yet fully realized in either heart or behavior – is one of the most grievous transgressions, and for some of us, the easiest to fall prey to. We need to attentively check this propensity if we wish to allow the creeper of love to grow without poisoning the garden with our own malice toward others.

Another offense is to be inattentive while chanting. Being distracted while chanting is a symptom that we suffer from material attachments and desires, or in other words, an unhealthy condition of heart. Our attachments don't dissolve immediately, but we want to be aware of the symptom – distraction in chanting – and its root cause and try our best to work on uprooting attachments to temporal matter. The more we endeavor in this way, the more we're able to approach the holy sound of the Name with respect, care, and focus.

If we remove laziness, restlessness, and indifference from our mantra meditation we will make rapid progress.

PADMA PURANA

Brahma Khanda 25.15–1

1. To criticize saintly persons (*sadhus*) who chant the holy name.
2. To think that other forms of divinity (Durga, Shiva, Ganesh, or any number of demigods) are equal to or independent of Bhagavan Sri Krishna.
3. To consider the guru who gives the Name an ordinary person, or to disobey the guru's instructions.
4. To minimize sacred texts that describe Krishna and the holy names.
5. To think that the glories and powers of the holy names have been exaggerated.
6. To interpret the meaning of the holy names without making reference to the texts that describe the holy names.
7. To sin with the idea that one will be absolved by chanting.
8. To equate the power of performing mundane pious activities or other "good" karmic activities to the power of chanting the holy names.
9. To teach the full glories of the Name to those who have no faith in the holy name.
10. To purposely maintain material attachments and thereby not develop full faith in the Name.

The *Padma Purana* ends, saying that inattention while chanting is also considered an offense. The *Purana* adds, "Only the holy name himself can remove the offenses of those who chant the Name with offenses. This happens for those who chant the Name constantly."

Hare Krishna
Hare Krishna
Krishna Krishna
Hare Hare
Hare Rama
Hare Rama
Rama Rama
Hare Hare

How to Chant Japa and Use a Bead Mala

What is a Bead Mala?

The word *mala* literally means "garland." A bead mala is a string of beads used to count mantras while chanting. Japa malas have been used for centuries in India for meditation and prayer – not so different from how prayer is counted in a number of other spiritual traditions on rosaries. Ideally, malas have 108 beads. 108 is an important number in Vedic astronomy, astrology, architecture, mathematics, and science and is considered sacred by other cultures and traditions as well. You'll also find malas with 27 beads. Counting four times around a 27-bead mala equals once around on a 108-bead mala.

Which Beads to Choose?

When purchasing a mala, choose beads made of tulsi wood over more expensive gemstone, sandalwood, or rudraksha beads. Tulsi is considered as the most sacred plant in Vedic culture, and especially in bhakti culture, and so yogis have used its wood for their prayer beads for millennia. When using tulsi mala, the word *mala* takes on special significance. Then *ma* means "wealth," and *la* means "gift." The tulasi mala gives the greatest wealth, that is, spiritual wealth. Tulsi also has many physical healing properties, and so touching the wood of tulsi is auspicious. If you're looking for the mystique or the energy benefits of a gemstone or other type of mala, remember that tulsi offers sacred benefits. In India, the tulsi plant is thought to protect its caregiver, and malas made of tulsi wood are beautiful, simple, spiritual, less expensive, and provide the mystique of participating in a very ancient practice.

Using Your Beads

(The QR code at the beginning of the appendixes will take you to a video of a demonstration of how to use the beads.)

All malas have a head bead. This is the largest bead and coming to it marks the completion of one round of japa. One does not chant on the head bead. Many yogis count a fixed number of rounds every day. Choose a number that works for you and recite your mantras daily. Most people who've become adept at japa find it takes anywhere from 5–8 minutes to chant the maha-mantra on 108 beads.

When chanting, use your right hand, as the left is considered unclean. Hold a bead between your thumb and middle finger or ring finger (which is the cleanest finger), and don't use your index finger. Most people find that rolling each bead gently between your fingers assists meditation by focusing the mind and makes counting easier. But you can also just hold the bead, too.

Recite the full mantra on each bead and then move to the next bead. When you reach the head bead, reverse your direction by chanting on the bead you just chanted on and then move to the next bead. In this way, you won't pass over the head bead and your next round of recitations will reverse the direction in which you just chanted.

The Meditation Technique

The practice of chanting a mantra quietly to oneself, usually with the aid of a mala, is called japa, and it's one form of maha-mantra yoga. You can sit, stand, or walk while chanting, though sitting often allows you to focus more. *The goal of japa meditation is to focus your attention completely on the mantra.*

Find a quiet, comfortable place, free from as many distractions as possible, for your meditation. You can use a seated yoga pose or just sit comfortably on the floor or a chair. What's important is that you sit in whatever way gives you the best chance at concentration. Don't get so comfortable you doze off, however. You can close your eyes to draw your attention inward or look at a picture as you chant – whatever helps control and focus the mind.

You'll likely discover that one time of day is better for focused chanting than another. Nearly all chanters report that chanting is easiest in the early morning – before the day gets busy and your mind along with it.

While chanting, when your mind wanders, gently bring it back to the mantra. Be prepared to do this over and over again. Fingering your beads can help you focus. As you practice controlling the mind and focusing on the mantra, the mind will gradually begin to cooperate more. Catch the mind when it drifts and bring it back as soon as you notice you're no longer hearing the mantra. In this way, you'll get the spiritual benefit of the mantra and the multiple physical and psychological side benefits of a meditation practice.

Adepts say that if you let the mind wander from the sound of the mantra and don't bring it back as soon as you've noticed its deviation, you'll develop a habit that's not only hard to change but will make staying with the meditation practice difficult. This is because when the mind wanders unrestricted and you don't hear the mantra, you get little taste while chanting and instead become bored. Not hearing the mantra means you don't experience it. You need to focus on the mantra and recite and hear it sincerely to get the results of chanting. If you insist that your mind focus, it will gradually comply.

You can chant as slowly or quickly as you like – whatever helps your focus while remaining clear in your recitation of the mantra.

Many people set an intention before they begin their meditation. We know intentions are powerful. They can draw us toward our goal and remind us of what we're trying to cultivate or accomplish. An intention, called a *sankalpa* in Sanskrit, can be a potent addition to your japa meditation. The goal of mantra meditation is to please the person in the mantra. In the maha-mantra, we find Radha and Krishna.

The maha-mantra is a transcendental vibration referred to as the "great chant for deliverance." By reciting the maha-mantra we petition to be released from the illusion of the false ego. We want to cleanse the mirror of the material mind so we can uncover our original identity as a unit of consciousness who has a relationship with our Divine Other.

The first word of the mantra, *Hare,* refers to the shakti of the Supreme, or Radha. The words *Krishna* and *Rama* are forms of directly addressing the Lord.

My teacher states that the chanting is a spiritual call for the Lord and his internal energy to give us protection. "The chanting is exactly like the genuine cry of a child for its mother. Mother Hara helps the devotee achieve the grace of Krishna, who reveals himself to one who chants this mantra sincerely. No other means of spiritual realization is as effective in this [cosmic] age as chanting the maha-mantra."

Hare Krishna, Hare Krishna
Krishna Krishna, Hare Hare
Hare Rama, Hare Rama
Rama Rama, Hare Hare

How to Store Your Mala

Keep your beads in a clean place. Many people leave them in their sacred space when not using them or use a japa mala bag. The bag has a hole for your index finger, which helps keep that finger off the beads. Be respectful of your beads. They shouldn't touch the floor, your feet, or any unclean place, or be taken into unclean places, like the bathroom.

Bibliography

Beck, Guy. *Sonic Liturgy: Ritual and Music in Hindu Tradition.* New Delhi, India: Dev Publishers & Distributors, 2014.
– *Sonic Theology: Hinduism and Sacred Sound.* Columbia, SC: University of South Carolina Press, 1993.
– *Sacred Sound: Experiencing Music in World Religions.* Waterloo, Ontario, Canada. Wilfrid Laurier University Press, 2006.
– "Divine Musical Instruments" in *Brill's Encyclopedia of Hinduism.* Retrieved October 24, 2020 from https://referenceworks. brillonline.com/entries/brill-s-encyclopedia-of-hinduism/ divine-musical-instruments-COM_000339
– "Kirtan and Bhajan" in *Brill's Encyclopedia of Hinduism.* Retrieved October 24, 2020 from https://referenceworks.brillonline.com/entries/ brill-s-encyclopedia-of-hinduism/kirtan-and-bhajan-COM_2040060

Bernard, Patrick. *Music as Yoga: Discover the Healing Power of Sound.* San Rafael, CA: Mandala Publishing, 2004.

Brahmachari, Mahanamabrata. *Vaisnava Vedanta.* Calcutta, India: Das Gupta & Co., 1974.

Bryant, Edwin F. *Bhakti Yoga: Tales and Teachings from the Bhagavata Purana.* New York, NY: North Point Press, 2017.

Comtois, Pranada. *Wise-Love: Bhakti and the Search for the Soul of Consciousness.* Gainesville: Chandra Media, 2018.
– *Bhakti Shakti: Goddess of Divine Love.* St. Augustine, FL: Chandra Media, 2022.

Dasa, Satyanarayana. Lecture series on the *Bhagavata Sandharbha* of Srila Jiva Gosvami from the Bhakti Tirtha Course. Vrindavan: Jiva Institute of Vaishnava Studies, 2018.

– Translation and commentary on *Sri Bhagavata Sandarbha* by Srila Jiva Gosvami. Vrindavan: Jiva Institute of Vaishnava Studies, 2014.
– Translation and commentary on *Sri Krsna Sandarbha* by Srila Jiva Gosvami. Vrindavan: Jiva Institute of Vaishnava Studies, 2018.

Das, Akhandadhi. "The Atma Paradigm" YouTube series. Retrieved November 10, 2020. https://www.youtube.com/c/TheAtmaParadigm

Goldberg, Philip. *American Veda: From Emerson and the Beatles to Yoga and Meditation, How Indian Spirituality Changed the West.* New York: Harmony Books, 2010.

Johnsen, Linda & Jacobus, Maggie. *Kirtan! Chanting as a Spiritual Path.* St. Paul, MN: Yes International Publishers, 2007.

Kuppusamy, Maheshkumar. "Effect of Mahamantra Chanting on Autonomic and Cognitive Functions- An Interventional Study" published in the *Journal of Clinical and Diagnostic Research*, May 2019. Accessed online 3 January 2022, https://www.researchgate.net/publication/332865596_Effect_of_Mahamantra_Chanting_on_Autonomic_and_Cognitive_Functions-_An_Interventional_Study

Le Mée, Katharine. *Chant: The Origins, Form, Practice, and Healing Power of Gregorian Chant.* New York: Bell Tower, 1994.

Paul, Russill. *The Yoga of Sound: Tapping the Hidden Power of Music and Chant.* Novato: New World Library, 2004.

Prime, Ranchor. *The Birth of Kirtan.* San Rafael, CA: Mandala Publishing, 2012.

Rosen, Steven, *The Yoga of Kirtan: Conversations on the Sacred Art of Chanting.* Nyack, New York: Folk Books, 2008.
– *Journal of Vaishnava Studies,* Volume 17, No 2. Poquoson, Virginia: Deepak Publishing, 2009.
– *Journal of Vaishnava Studies,* Volume 24, No 2. Nyack, New York: Folk Books, 2016.
– *Sonic Spirituality: A Collection of Essays on the Hare Krishna Maha-mantra.* Vrindavan: Rasabihari Alok and Sons, 2009.

Sexton, Shannon & Dubrovsky, Anna. "The Kirtan Revolution Brings an Ancient Practice to a Modern World." *Yoga Journal*. Retrieved October 22, 2020, from https://www.yogajournal.com/lifestyle/sing-soul-electric

Sinha, Nandalal. *The Bhakti Sutras of Narada.* Allahabad: The Panini Office Bhuvanesvari Asrama, 1917.

Snodgrass, Cynthia, *Sonic Thread: Sound as a Pathway to Spirituality.* New York: Paraview Press, 2002.

Swami, A. C. Bhaktivedanta Prabhupada. *Bhagavad-gita As It Is.* Sanskrit text, translation and commentary. Los Angeles: The Bhaktivedanta Book Trust, 1980.
– *Sri Caitanya-caritamrta.* Bengali text, translation and commentary. Los Angeles: The Bhaktivedanta Book Trust, 1996.
– *Srimad-Bhagavatam.* [Bhagavata Purana] Sanskrit text, translation and commentary. Los Angeles: The Bhaktivedanta Book Trust, 1978.

Swami B.B. Tirtha and Swami B.V. Tripurari, *Bhajan: Mantras of Mercy.* Novato: Mandala Publishing, 2002.

Swami, Bhakti Kamal Tyagi. *Sri Sri Upadesamrta* by Rupa Gosvami with commentaries by Bhakti Vinod Thakur, Bhakti Siddhanta Saraswati Thakur, B. R. Sridar Dev-Goswami, translation. Felham: Sri Chaitanya Saraswat Math, 2019.

Swami, Sacinandana, *The Living Name: A Guide to Chanting with Absorption,* Germany: Saranagati Publishing, 2018.

Thakura, Bhaktivinoda. *Sri Sanmodana Bhasyam* with commentary by Bhaktisiddhanta Sarasvati Thakura. Retrieved December 12, 2020, from http://ebooks.iskcondesiretree.com/pdf/Gaudiya_Books%20/Bhaktivinoda_Thakura/Bhaktivinoda_Thakura_Sri_Sanmodana_Bhasyam.pdf
– *Sri Caitanya-siksamrta* translated by Bhanu Swami. Vrindavan, India: Brhat Mrdanga Press, 2004.

Thakura, Sri Nayanananda. *Sri Sri Preyo-Bhakti-Rasarnava.* Translation by Dasaratha-Suta Dasa. Charlottesville, VA: Bookwrights Press, 2018.

Tripurari, Swami. *Bhagavad Gita: Its Feeling and Philosophy.* San Rafael: Mandala Publishing, 2010.
– *Siksastakam of Sri Caitanya.* San Rafael: Mandala Publishing, 2005.
– "Where Shakti Rules." Harmonist. Retrieved June 29, 2022, from https://harmonist.us/2022/06/where-shakti-rules/.

Vilhauer Ph.D., Jennice. "Kirtan: The Easy Meditation That Can Improve Your Brain." *Psychology Today.* Retrieved October 22, 2020, from https://www.psychologytoday.com/us/blog/living-forward/201812/kirtan-the-easy-meditation-can-improve-your-brain.

Whitehurst, Richard. *Mahamantra Yoga: Chanting to Anchor the Mind and Access the Divine.* Rochester: Destiny Books, 2011.

ACKNOWLEDGMENTS

I'm compelled by affection to start by thanking my dear friend and lifelong partner, Nagaraja dasa, who made this book possible by taking up many of my responsibilities in the home. Thank you, Nag, for your undying support and all the ways you make life manageable. I so appreciate being able to walk to the door of your home office and ask any question I have about a word choice or editing problem, or to tell you about one of the many magical things that just occurred while writing. It is a joy to have you in my life.

Thank you Deva Madhava, Mahendra, and Rasa Sthali for reading the rough manuscript. By tolerating the work at that stage and giving me critical feedback you each contributed significantly to the finished work. I'm so grateful for your help and friendship.

I offer a very special thanks to Jessica Karpiak. Jess, your attention to detail and sensitive comments about how to improve a key area of the book brought *Prema Kirtan* to another level. Thank you for taking time out of your busy schedule to lend your perceptive insights and detailed comments.

Kaisori, I remain indebted to you for editing though you're actually overly-busy as a sought-after editor. You have a keen ability to uplift a work. I can't imagine writing a book without you.

I'm grateful to Kosa Ely, who is forever willing to brainstorm with me on any issue. Kosa, your artistic sensibilities, publishing vision, and enthusiastic support have made my writing and publishing journey possible, and you've brightened many cloudy days with your optimistic perspectives. Thank you for always being ready to take the next step with me.

I humbly bow to my spiritual masters who removed darkness and sorrow from my heart, opened my eyes to my spiritual nature and prospect, and filled me with the wealth of bhakti.

About the Author

Pranada Comtois is a devoted pilgrim who sheds light on Bhakti, the path of loving devotion, which is known as the heart and soul of yoga. She is a featured speaker in the film *Women of Bhakti*. Her first book, *Wise-Love: Bhakti and the Search for the Soul of Consciousness,* won multiple awards, including the 2019 Montaigne Medal given "for the most thought-provoking books that illuminate, progress, or redirect thought." Her second book *Bhakti-Shakti: Goddess of Divine Love,* placed as a finalist in two publishing awards, and is the first book about Sri Radha, the hidden secret of the Upanishads, written for a Western audience. She lives in Florida with her husband and is working on the fourth book in The Bhakti Series. You can contact Pranada at pranadacomtois.com.

Printed in Great Britain
by Amazon

16236094R00125